Eritreans' Evolution

The Path to Transformation

Mohammed Zara

Eritreans' Evolution:

The Path to Transformation

ISBN: 9798871508107

Book design by

MBD

Table contents

Chapters briefly,

Chapter 1: The Tapestry of Eritrean Life

In the heart of the Horn of Africa lies Eritrea, a nation with a rich cultural heritage and a tumultuous history. This book delves into the multifaceted challenges faced by Eritreans, both within the country and across the diaspora.

Chapter 2: Historical Perspective

To understand the present struggles of Eritreans, we must first explore the historical context. From Italian colonization to British administration and Ethiopian annexation, Eritrea has faced a series of external influences that shaped its destiny. The struggle for independence culminated in 1993, with Eritrea gaining sovereignty. However, the challenges were far from over.

Chapter 3: Governance Systems and Economic Struggles

A crucial aspect of Eritrea's challenges lies in its governance systems. The centralized, authoritarian rule under President Isaias

Afwerki has led to limited political freedoms, economic stagnation, and widespread poverty. The book examines the policies that have hindered development and triggered a mass exodus of Eritreans seeking a better life abroad.

Chapter 4: Eritrean Diaspora

As Eritreans fled their homeland, they formed a vast diaspora scattered across the globe. This chapter explores the stories of resilience, sacrifice, and hope as Eritreans navigate the challenges of building new lives in foreign lands.

Chapter 5: Impact on Families and Communities

The separation caused by migration has profound effects on Eritrean families. From the strain of long-distance relationships to the financial burden of supporting loved ones back home, the diaspora's impact on families is a central theme in this chapter.

Chapter 6: Activism and Advocacy

Despite the physical distance from their homeland, Eritreans abroad are actively engaged in advocacy and activism. This chapter sheds light on the efforts to raise awareness about the challenges faced by Eritreans and to influence international policies for positive change.

Chapter 7: The Failures of Dictatorship

The dictatorship in Eritrea has stifled dissent, suppressed free speech, and violated human rights. This chapter delves into the consequences of authoritarian rule, both within the country and for Eritreans living abroad.

Chapter 8: Toward a Better Future

Amidst the challenges, there is hope. This chapter explores the aspirations and initiatives of Eritreans working toward a better future for their country. From grassroots movements to international collaborations, the book highlights the paths that could lead to positive change.

Epilogue: A Collective Journey

In the closing chapter, the book reflects on the collective journey of Eritreans, both within the country and in the diaspora. It explores the possibilities for a more inclusive and prosperous

Eritrea, shaped by the resilience and determination of its people.

Introduction

In the shadows of hardship and the echoes of perseverance lies a profound narrative—the story of Eritrea and its indomitable people. "Enduring Struggle: Eritreans' Path to Change" is a testament to the resilience, courage, and unwavering spirit that defines the collective journey toward transformation.

From the quiet determination of individuals to the communal resilience forged through trials, this book unravels the intricate tapestry woven by the Eritrean people. It is a chronicle that transcends borders, capturing the essence of a nation's unwavering pursuit of change, one steeped in the aspirations and sacrifices of its citizens.

Through the lens of countless narratives, this book embarks on a profound exploration—a journey that navigates through the labyrinth of challenges, hopes, and aspirations that have shaped the Eritrean landscape. It unveils the untold stories of bravery, the unspoken dreams that fuel an enduring struggle, and the relentless pursuit of a future brimming with promise.

"Enduring Struggle" is not just a retelling of historical events; it is a living testament to the resilience of a people bound by their yearning for change. It invites you to walk alongside Eritrea's sons and daughters, to witness their unwavering dedication, and to grasp the profound significance of their path to change—a path etched with fortitude, unity, and an unyielding spirit.

Chapter One

The Tapestry of Eritrean Life

In the intricate tapestry of Eritrean life, threads of resilience, tradition, and struggle are tightly woven together, forming a narrative that spans generations. Eritrea, nestled along the Red Sea coast, has a cultural heritage as diverse as its landscapes – from the highlands of Asmara to the lowlands of the Danakil Depression. This chapter explores the rich tapestry of Eritrean life, delving into the traditions, values, and historical legacies that have shaped the identity of its people.

The Cultural Kaleidoscope

Eritrea is a mosaic of ethnic groups, each contributing unique hues to the nation's cultural palette. Tigrinya, Tigre, Saho, Bilen, Afar, and other languages weave a linguistic tapestry that mirrors the country's diversity. From vibrant traditional attire to spirited dance forms, the cultural richness of Eritrea is a testament to the resilience of its people.

Echoes of History

The historical journey of Eritrea is etched into the fabric of its society. Italian colonization, British administration, and the struggle for independence have left indelible marks. The echoes of battles fought in the mountains resonate with the spirit of freedom that courses through the veins of every Eritrean.

Resilience in Adversity

Eritreans have faced numerous challenges throughout history – from the scars of war to the hardships of a fledgling nation. Yet, their resilience shines through. The agricultural communities in the highlands, the nomadic tribes in the lowlands, and the bustling urban life in Asmara all reflect a people who have weathered storms with grace and determination.

Family and Community Bonds

At the heart of Eritrean life is a deep sense of community and familial bonds. Extended families provide a support network that extends beyond blood relations, embodying the proverb, "እዛ ናይ ቱዛ" ("One hand washes the other"). This interconnectedness sustains Eritrean communities, fostering a sense of shared identity.

The Lure of the Land

The diverse geography of Eritrea, encompassing mountains, plains, and coastline, has shaped the way of life for its people. The agrarian practices in the highlands, the nomadic herding in the lowlands, and the maritime traditions along the Red Sea all contribute to the multifaceted identity of Eritrea.

Threads of Identity

Eritrean identity is a tapestry interwoven with pride in cultural heritage and a determination to forge ahead. Whether in the bustling markets of Asmara or the quiet villages dotting the countryside, the threads of identity are tightly knit, creating a sense of unity that transcends the challenges faced by the nation.

As we unravel the threads of Eritrean life, we begin to understand the complexities and beauty of a nation that has navigated a tumultuous history while holding onto the threads of its cultural identity. In the following chapters, we will explore how these threads are tested as Eritreans confront the challenges that have altered the course of their lives and dispersed them across the globe.

The Cultural Kaleidoscope

Eritrea, with its diverse ethnic groups and languages, is a cultural kaleidoscope where traditions, languages, and customs blend harmoniously to create a vibrant tapestry of identity. Each community contributes distinct colors and patterns to this cultural mosaic, enriching the collective heritage of the nation.

Linguistic Diversity

Eritrea's linguistic landscape reflects the plurality of its people. Tigrinya, spoken by the majority, is the official language. Tigre, Saho, Bilen, Afar, and other languages add further layers to this linguistic tapestry. These languages are not merely modes of communication but vessels carrying the stories, wisdom, and traditions of each community.

Traditional Attire and Adornments

The traditional attire of Eritreans is a visual testament to the rich cultural diversity. From the elaborate Tigrinya dresses with intricate embroidery to the vibrant patterns of the Tigre and Saho communities, traditional clothing is more than adornment; it's a celebration of heritage. Adornments like jewelry and hairstyles also hold cultural significance, reflecting a deep connection to history and identity.

Culinary Traditions

Eritrean cuisine is a gastronomic delight that mirrors the nation's diversity. Injera, a sourdough flatbread, is a staple, often accompanied by a variety of stews and vegetables. Each ethnic group brings its own unique flavors and cooking techniques to the table, creating a culinary experience that is both diverse and delicious.

Dance and Music

Dance and music are integral to Eritrean cultural expression. Traditional dances, like the Tigrinya and Saho, are not just performances but expressions of joy, sorrow, and community bonding. Musical genres, ranging from the soulful Tigrigna songs to the rhythmic beats of the Afar, embody the spirit of the people and their shared experiences.

Religious Practices

Religious diversity is another facet of Eritrea's cultural kaleidoscope. The majority of Eritreans practice Orthodox Christianity or Islam, with various denominations and sects coexisting peacefully. Religious festivals and ceremonies play a crucial role in shaping the cultural calendar, fostering unity among diverse religious communities.

Oral Traditions and Storytelling

The oral tradition is a cornerstone of Eritrean culture, where stories, proverbs, and fables are passed down through generations. Elders play a vital role as custodians of wisdom, ensuring that the collective memory of the community remains alive. These narratives not only entertain but also serve as moral guides and historical records.

Cultural Festivals

Throughout the year, Eritreans come together to celebrate cultural festivals that showcase the richness of their heritage. From the vibrant Keren Festival to the solemn observances of religious holidays, these events provide a platform for communities to express their identity, share traditions, and strengthen social bonds.

In this cultural kaleidoscope, the diversity of Eritrea's people is not a source of division but a testament to the resilience and unity that define the nation. As we explore the challenges faced by Eritreans, it's essential to appreciate the cultural foundation that sustains them, even in the face of adversity.

Echoes of History

The echoes of Eritrea's history reverberate through time, telling a tale of resilience, resistance, and the pursuit of freedom. From the shores of the Red Sea to the mountainous highlands, every landscape bears witness to the struggles and triumphs that have shaped Eritrea into the nation it is today.

Italian Colonization

The late 19th century saw Eritrea fall under Italian colonization, marking the beginning of a period that would leave an indelible mark on the nation. Asmara, the capital, became a showcase for Italian architecture, with art deco buildings dotting the cityscape. The remnants of this colonial era, from architecture to cultural influences, are still visible today, a testament to Eritrea's ability to absorb and adapt.

British Administration

After World War II, the British administration took control of Eritrea, introducing a different chapter in the nation's history. The push for self-determination began to gain momentum, setting the stage for the struggles that would follow. The influences of this era are evident in the administrative structures and educational systems that laid the groundwork for a nascent Eritrean identity.

Struggle for Independence

The quest for independence emerged as a defining theme in Eritrea's history, culminating in a protracted armed struggle that lasted for three decades. The Eritrean People's Liberation

Front (EPLF) played a pivotal role in challenging Ethiopian rule. The mountains, once silent witnesses to centuries of history, became the battlegrounds where Eritreans fought for their right to self-determination.

Birth of a Nation

The resilience of the Eritrean people bore fruit in 1993 when the nation finally gained its independence. As the flag was raised in Asmara, it marked the end of a long and arduous journey. Eritrea emerged as a sovereign state, but the challenges were far from over. Rebuilding a nation shattered by war required not only physical reconstruction but also the healing of wounds and the forging of a new national identity.

Ethiopian Annexation and Struggle

Before independence, Eritrea endured a painful chapter of annexation by Ethiopia. The period from 1952 to 1991 saw Eritreans resisting Ethiopian rule, with the struggle reaching its peak in the later years. The scars of this annexation run deep, shaping the collective memory and determination of a people who fought against oppression.

War with Ethiopia

The early years of Eritrea's independence were marred by a bitter conflict with Ethiopia over border disputes. The two-year war, which ended in 2000, took a toll on both nations. The echoes of this conflict linger, reminding Eritreans of the fragility of peace and the need for vigilance in safeguarding their hard-won sovereignty.

As we listen to the echoes of history, we gain insight into the challenges that have molded the Eritrean identity. The scars and triumphs, etched into the very fabric of the nation, set the stage for the contemporary struggles faced by Eritreans within their borders and around the world.

Resilience in Adversity

In the face of formidable challenges, Eritreans have exemplified a remarkable resilience that defines their spirit. From the ravages of war to the hardships of nation-building, the people of Eritrea have drawn strength from their deep-rooted sense of community, cultural heritage, and an unwavering commitment to a better future.

War and Its Aftermath

The prolonged struggle for independence and subsequent conflicts have left enduring scars on the landscape and psyche of Eritrea. The resilience of its people, however, is evident in the efforts to rebuild shattered communities and infrastructure. Villages destroyed during the war have been reconstructed, and agricultural lands, once battlegrounds, have been revitalized through collective endeavors.

Agricultural Resilience

The predominantly agrarian communities in the highlands of Eritrea have faced the challenges of arid conditions and erratic rainfall. Despite these adversities, Eritrean farmers have employed innovative agricultural practices, such as terracing and water conservation, to cultivate the land sustainably. The resilience of these communities is reflected in their ability to adapt to environmental challenges and ensure food security.

Urban Renewal in Asmara

Asmara, the capital city, bears witness to a different manifestation of Eritrean resilience. The city, with its well-preserved Italian colonial architecture, reflects the determination of its inhabitants to maintain a connection to their history. The resilience of Asmara extends beyond the physical structures; it encompasses a commitment to preserving cultural heritage and fostering a sense of continuity amid change.

Nation-Building Endeavors

The post-independence period demanded a new kind of resilience as Eritrea embarked on the arduous journey of nation-building. The challenges were immense, from establishing governmental institutions to creating economic stability. Eritreans, however, embraced these challenges with determination, working collectively to lay the foundations for a sovereign and self-reliant nation.

Education as a Catalyst

Education has been a cornerstone of Eritrea's resilience, serving as a catalyst for progress and empowerment. Despite resource constraints, the commitment to providing education for all has been unwavering. Schools and educational programs have flourished, contributing to the intellectual capital that is essential for the nation's development.

Social Cohesion

Perhaps the most profound demonstration of Eritrean resilience is the social cohesion that binds communities together. Extended families, neighborhood networks, and communal support systems have been instrumental in helping individuals navigate challenges. In times of adversity, Eritreans have leaned on these social bonds, creating a safety net that transcends economic or political hardships.

Hope Amidst Hardship

Eritreans, whether in the highlands cultivating the land or in the urban centers striving for economic stability, embody a spirit of hope amidst hardship. It is this hope that fuels their resilience, propelling them forward in the face of adversity and inspiring future generations to continue the journey toward a brighter and more prosperous Eritrea.

As we explore the resilience ingrained in the fabric of Eritrean life, we recognize that it is not merely a response to challenges but a foundational element of their identity. The resilience of Eritrea and its people serves as a beacon of inspiration, illuminating the path toward a future defined by strength, unity, and the pursuit of a better tomorrow.

Family and Community Bonds

In the intricate fabric of Eritrean life, the strength of family and community bonds stands as a resilient thread that weaves together the social fabric of the nation. These bonds, characterized by a deep sense of interconnectedness and mutual support, play a pivotal role in shaping the identity and resilience of the Eritrean people.

Extended Families as Pillars of Support

The concept of family in Eritrea extends beyond the nuclear unit to encompass extended families and kinship networks. The bonds forged within these extended families serve as pillars of emotional, financial, and social support. Whether in times of celebration or adversity, the collective strength of the extended family provides a safety net that bolsters individuals and ensures that no one faces life's challenges alone.

Intergenerational Wisdom

Eritrean communities value the wisdom passed down through generations. Elders hold a revered place within families and communities, serving as repositories of knowledge, tradition, and cultural heritage. The intergenerational exchange of wisdom not only preserves the rich tapestry of Eritrean culture but also imparts valuable lessons that guide younger generations in navigating life's complexities.

Communal Celebrations and Mourning

Life's milestones are communal affairs in Eritrea. From weddings and births to religious celebrations and funerals, the community plays an integral role in these events. The collective participation in both joyous and somber occasions fosters a sense of shared identity and reinforces the notion that individual experiences are inseparable from the broader tapestry of community life.

Economic Cooperation and Mutual Aid

Economic challenges are often addressed collectively within Eritrean communities. The practice of "hawashay," a form of community labor where individuals come together to help a neighbor with agricultural work or construction projects, exemplifies the spirit of mutual aid. This not only eases the burden on individual households but also reinforces the interconnectedness that defines Eritrean communities.

Migration and Transnational Families

The Eritrean diaspora, a result of migration driven by various factors, has reshaped the dynamics of family bonds. Despite physical distances, transnational families remain deeply connected through regular communication, financial support, and a shared commitment to preserving cultural traditions. The diaspora becomes an extension of the Eritrean community, contributing to the resilience of both those at home and abroad.

Women as Pillars of Family Strength

Eritrean women play a central role in maintaining family and community bonds. Their contributions to agriculture, education, and community well-being are significant. Women often serve as the backbone of extended families, embodying strength, resilience, and nurturing care that sustains the social fabric of Eritrean communities.

Social Cohesion in Neighborhoods

Beyond family ties, Eritrean communities are characterized by strong social cohesion within neighborhoods. The concept of "she'eb" refers to the practice of neighbors coming together to solve common problems or celebrate shared successes. This sense of neighborhood solidarity further enhances the interconnectedness that defines Eritrean community life.

In exploring the intricate relationships within families and communities, it becomes evident that they form the bedrock of Eritrean society. As we continue to unravel the challenges faced by Eritreans, the enduring strength of these bonds serves as a source of inspiration and resilience, illuminating a path forward rooted in shared values and collective support.

The Lure of the Land

Eritrea's diverse and captivating landscapes, ranging from the fertile highlands to the arid lowlands and the pristine coastline along the Red Sea, exert a powerful allure that has shaped the way of life for its people. The connection between the Eritrean people and their land is not merely geographical; it is a profound and symbiotic relationship that influences cultural practices, livelihoods, and the very essence of identity.

Agrarian Life in the Highlands

The highlands of Eritrea, with their cool temperatures and fertile soil, have long been the heartland of agrarian life. Terraced fields adorn the slopes, where farmers cultivate crops such as barley, wheat, and teff. The traditional method of terracing not only maximizes arable land but also serves as a testament to the ingenuity of Eritrean agricultural practices, adapting to the challenges posed by the mountainous terrain.

Nomadic Herding in the Lowlands

Contrasting the highlands, the lowlands of Eritrea present a vast expanse of arid landscapes. Nomadic herding communities, such as the Afar and Bilen, have thrived in these challenging conditions. Herding goats, sheep, and camels, these communities have developed a unique relationship with the land, relying on the mobility of their lifestyles to navigate changing grazing patterns and seasonal variations.

Maritime Traditions along the Red Sea

The Red Sea, with its crystal-clear waters and abundant marine life, has been a source of sustenance and economic activity for coastal communities. Fishing villages dot the coastline, where traditional fishing methods are employed alongside modern techniques. The Red Sea not only provides a livelihood but also serves as a cultural focal point, influencing cuisine, folklore, and artistic expressions.

Urban Centers and Economic Hubs

The lure of the land extends to urban centers, notably Asmara, where the convergence of diverse landscapes is reflected in the city's architecture, lifestyle, and economic activities. Asmara, a UNESCO World Heritage site, showcases a unique blend of Italian colonial, art deco, and modernist architecture. The city's vibrant markets and bustling streets capture the dynamism that arises from the intersection of rural and urban influences.

Spiritual Connection to the Land

Eritrean spirituality is intricately connected to the land. Sacred sites, such as monasteries in the highlands or revered natural formations, hold profound significance. Pilgrimages to these sites, often undertaken as communal endeavors, reinforce the spiritual bond between the Eritrean people and their land, fostering a sense of reverence and continuity.

Environmental Stewardship

The lure of the land is not just about extraction but also about preservation. Eritreans, rooted in a deep respect for nature, have practiced sustainable agricultural methods and water conservation for generations. Traditional ecological knowledge, passed down through communities, underscores the importance of maintaining harmony with the environment.

Challenges and Adaptations

While the land has been a source of sustenance and cultural richness, it has also presented challenges. Climate variability, desertification, and water scarcity pose threats to livelihoods. Eritreans, however, have displayed resilience by adapting traditional practices, embracing modern technologies, and implementing community-based conservation efforts.

In the allure of the land, Eritrea finds its identity—a dynamic interplay between the people and the diverse ecosystems they call home. As we delve into the challenges faced by Eritreans, understanding this profound connection to the land becomes crucial, as it shapes their responses to adversities and informs the path toward a sustainable and prosperous future.

Threads of Identity

In the intricate tapestry of Eritrean life, the threads of identity are tightly woven, creating a rich and diverse pattern that reflects the nation's history, culture, and the collective experiences of its people. These threads, symbolic of the resilience and unity that define Eritrean identity, are shaped by a deep connection to the land, a complex history of struggle, and a commitment to cultural heritage.

Cultural Diversity as a Tapestry

Eritrea's identity is a mosaic of cultures, languages, and traditions. Each ethnic group contributes a unique thread to the fabric of the nation, creating a vibrant and harmonious tapestry. The Tigrinya, Tigre, Saho, Bilen, Afar, and other communities bring their distinct colors and patterns, fostering a sense of unity amid diversity.

Language as an Expressive Thread

Language is a fundamental thread in Eritrea's identity. Tigrinya, the most widely spoken language, serves as a linguistic cornerstone, while Tigre, Saho, Bilen, and other languages contribute their own linguistic richness. The diverse languages encapsulate the stories, proverbs, and expressions that form the oral tradition, passing down the collective wisdom of Eritrean communities.

Symbols of Resilience

Historical symbols, such as the Martyrs Memorial in Asmara, stand as threads of resilience in the Eritrean identity. The memorial, dedicated to those who sacrificed their lives for independence, represents a collective commitment to freedom and the enduring spirit of the Eritrean people.

Independence as a Unifying Thread

The achievement of independence in 1993 serves as a unifying thread that runs through the fabric of Eritrean identity. The struggle for self-determination, symbolized by the Eritrean People's Liberation Front (EPLF) and its iconic flag, is a testament to the resilience and determination of a people who fought against oppression.

Religious Harmony

Religious diversity, another integral thread, is woven into the very fabric of Eritrean identity. Christians and Muslims coexist harmoniously, contributing to a national identity that transcends religious differences. The celebration of religious festivals, such as Christmas and Eid, is a shared experience that strengthens the bonds of unity.

Connection to the Land

The connection to the land forms a foundational thread in Eritrean identity. Whether in the highlands cultivating crops, the lowlands practicing nomadic herding, or along the Red Sea engaging in fishing, the diverse landscapes are integral to the identity of the Eritrean people. The land, with its mountains, plains, and coastline, shapes cultural practices, economic activities, and a profound sense of belonging.

Diaspora as a Global Thread

The Eritrean diaspora, dispersed across the globe, contributes a global thread to the nation's identity. Eritreans abroad, while adapting to new environments, actively maintain their cultural heritage, participate in diaspora communities, and engage in transnational efforts to support their homeland.

Resilience as a Common Thread

Resilience is the common thread that runs through the entirety of Eritrean identity. From historical struggles to the challenges of nation-building and the complexities faced by the diaspora, the unwavering spirit of resilience defines the character of the Eritrean people.

In exploring the threads of identity, we unravel a narrative of diversity, strength, and unity that forms the essence of Eritrea. As the nation confronts contemporary challenges, these threads serve as a source of inspiration, guiding the way toward a future that embraces the richness of its identity while navigating the complexities of a rapidly changing world.

Chapter Two

Historical Perspective

In the annals of Eritrea's history, a saga unfolds that encompasses centuries of resilience, external influences, and the relentless pursuit of sovereignty. To comprehend the challenges faced by Eritreans today, we embark on a historical journey, navigating through periods of colonization, foreign rule, and the protracted struggle for independence.

Italian Colonization: Shaping the Landscape

The late 19th century witnessed the arrival of Italian colonizers on the shores of the Red Sea. Eritrea became an Italian colony in 1890, and Asmara, the capital, transformed into a showcase for Italian architecture. The legacy of Italian influence endures in the city's art deco buildings and the cultural tapestry of Eritrea. Italian colonization not only left physical imprints on the landscape but also sparked a resistance that laid the groundwork for the struggle for self-determination.

British Administration: A Temporary Interlude

Following Italy's defeat in World War II, the British administered Eritrea from 1941 to 1952. This period was marked by attempts to balance the desires for Eritrean independence with the strategic interests of the global powers. The British administration laid the groundwork for educational institutions and administrative structures, setting the stage for the challenges that would follow.

Ethiopian Annexation: A Painful Chapter

The dream of Eritrean independence was deferred when, in 1952, the United Nations federated Eritrea with Ethiopia. This arrangement, intended to be temporary, quickly unraveled as Ethiopia sought to assimilate Eritrea. The annexation in 1962 marked the beginning of a dark chapter in Eritrea's history. The Ethiopian government's attempts to suppress Eritrean identity and language fueled discontent and sowed the seeds of resistance.

Armed Struggle: The Birth of the EPLF

Frustration with Ethiopian rule culminated in the birth of the Eritrean People's Liberation Front (EPLF) in the early 1970s. The armed struggle for independence became a defining period in Eritrea's history. The rugged mountains and vast deserts served as the battlegrounds where Eritreans fought for their right to self-determination. The struggle garnered international attention and support, with the EPLF becoming a symbol of resistance and hope.

Independence: A Hard-Fought Victory

After a protracted and bloody conflict, Eritrea achieved independence in 1993. The raising of the Eritrean flag in Asmara marked the end of a journey characterized by sacrifice, resilience, and unwavering determination. Independence, however, did not usher in an era of unbridled prosperity; it presented a new set of challenges as the nation sought to rebuild and redefine its identity on the world stage.

Border Conflict with Ethiopia: A Fragile Peace

The euphoria of independence was tempered by the outbreak of war with Ethiopia in 1998 over border disputes. The conflict, which lasted until 2000, resulted in significant human and economic costs for both nations. The subsequent peace agreements did not completely erase tensions, leaving a delicate peace that continues to influence regional dynamics.

Authoritarian Governance: A Struggle for Democracy

Post-independence Eritrea faced challenges associated with authoritarian rule. President Isaias Afwerki's government, while consolidating power, limited political freedoms and suppressed dissent. The struggles for democracy and human rights became defining features of Eritrea's contemporary history, influencing the diaspora's activism and shaping international perceptions.

As we delve into Eritrea's historical perspective, we encounter a narrative of endurance, resistance, and the quest for self-determination. The threads of this history intertwine with the challenges faced by Eritreans today, providing crucial context for understanding their journey and aspirations for a better future.

Italian Colonization: Shaping the Landscape

In the late 19th century, the arrival of Italian colonizers marked a transformative chapter in Eritrea's history, leaving an indelible imprint on the landscape, culture, and trajectory of the nation. The Italian presence, spanning from 1890 to 1941, not only shaped the physical infrastructure but also fueled a resistance that laid the groundwork for Eritrea's eventual pursuit of independence.

Asmara's Architectural Legacy

The most visible legacy of Italian colonization can be found in Asmara, Eritrea's capital. Italian architects infused the city with a distinctive blend of art deco, futurist, and colonial architectural styles. Asmara's streets are lined with elegant buildings, broad boulevards, and grand theaters that stand as a testament to Italian influence. The cityscape itself narrates the story of an era when Eritrea became a showcase for Italian urban planning and design.

Economic Developments and Infrastructure

The Italians invested in economic developments that transformed Eritrea's infrastructure. Modern transportation networks, including the construction of the Eritrean Railway, connected Asmara to the port city of Massawa. The development of roads and bridges facilitated access to remote regions, stimulating economic activities and trade. These infrastructural improvements laid the groundwork for a more interconnected and accessible Eritrea.

Cultural Exchange and Linguistic Impact

Italian colonization brought about a cultural exchange that left an enduring impact on Eritrean society. The Italian language became a part of the linguistic tapestry, influencing education, administration, and daily life. While Tigrinya, Tigre, and other local languages remained prevalent, the Italian linguistic influence is still evident in various aspects of Eritrean culture, from culinary terms to architectural terminology.

Indigenous Resistance: Seeds of Independence

The era of Italian colonization also sowed the seeds of resistance among the indigenous population. Eritreans, facing discrimination and exploitation, began to organize and resist foreign rule. The seeds of nationalism were planted during this period, culminating in the Eritrean War of Independence as a response to subsequent attempts at annexation and subjugation.

Legacy of Racial Policies

Italian racial policies, especially during the fascist era, left a dark legacy. The imposition of racial hierarchies and discriminatory practices engendered deep-seated resentments. The scars of these policies persisted, contributing to Eritrea's determination to assert its independence and affirm its identity in the face of external influences.

Liberation Movements: Eritrea's Struggle Begins

As the winds of World War II shifted, Italian forces were ousted from Eritrea by British and Allied troops in 1941. This marked the end of

Italian colonial rule, but it also set the stage for subsequent struggles for self-determination. The vacuum left by the departing colonizers became a catalyst for Eritrean aspirations and laid the groundwork for the complex historical journey that would follow.

Italian colonization, with its architectural, economic, and cultural influences, played a pivotal role in shaping Eritrea's landscape. However, it was the resistance against colonial rule that laid the foundation for Eritrea's determined pursuit of independence, marking the beginning of a historical narrative characterized by resilience and a quest for self-determination.

British Administration: A Temporary Interlude

In the aftermath of World War II, Eritrea found itself under the administration of the British military, marking a brief but consequential chapter in its history. The period from 1941 to 1952, although intended as a temporary interlude, played a pivotal role in shaping the trajectory of Eritrea's journey toward self-determination and independence.

Liberation from Italian Rule

With the defeat of Italian forces in Eritrea in 1941, the British assumed control of the territory as part of the broader Allied efforts during World War II. Eritrea, liberated from Italian colonial rule, faced a transitional period as the international community grappled with the question of its political future.

United Nations Trusteeship

In 1950, the United Nations (UN) declared Eritrea a federated state with Ethiopia, aiming to provide the nation with a form of self-governance under Ethiopian oversight. This decision, driven by geopolitical considerations and the strategic interests of the global powers, set the stage for a complex political landscape.

Educational and Administrative Developments

During the British administration, efforts were made to modernize Eritrea's educational and administrative systems. Schools were established, and an attempt was made to provide the population with access to education. Additionally, administrative structures were put in place, contributing to the development of institutions that would later play a role in post-independence Eritrea.

Tensions and Discontent

The hopes for a smooth transition to self-determination were quickly dashed as tensions between Eritrean aspirations and Ethiopian interests emerged. Eritreans, having experienced the brief period of British administration, harbored expectations of a future free from external control. However, the evolving geopolitical landscape and strategic interests of Ethiopia complicated the path to genuine self-determination.

Abrogation of the UN Plan

In 1952, the UN's plan for Eritrea's federation with Ethiopia began to unravel. The Ethiopian government, led by Emperor Haile Selassie, sought to absorb Eritrea into its fold, dismissing the notion of Eritrean independence. This abrogation of the UN plan marked the beginning of a turbulent era for Eritrea, as it faced the prospect of annexation and loss of the autonomy that many had hoped for.

Seeds of Dissent and the Road to Independence

The abrogation of the UN plan sowed the seeds of discontent among Eritreans and fueled the resistance movement. The desire for self-determination and independence gained momentum, laying the groundwork for the Eritrean People's Liberation Front (EPLF) and other movements that would later lead the armed struggle for liberation.

Legacy of British Administration

The legacy of the British administration in Eritrea is complex. While there were attempts to modernize and provide access to education, the geopolitical realities of the time, coupled with the subsequent abrogation of the UN plan, set the stage for a protracted struggle for independence. The period highlighted the challenges of international intervention and the delicate balance between global politics and the aspirations of a people.

As Eritrea transitioned from Italian colonization to British administration, the hopes for self-determination faced challenges on the geopolitical stage. The decisions made during this temporary interlude laid the groundwork for the complexities that would follow, setting Eritrea on a path toward a prolonged struggle for true autonomy and independence.

Ethiopian Annexation: A Painful Chapter

The post-World War II period marked a painful and tumultuous chapter in Eritrea's history, as the United Nations' initial plan for self-determination gave way to the annexation of Eritrea by Ethiopia in 1952. This annexation, orchestrated by Emperor Haile Selassie, unfolded against the will of the Eritrean people, setting the stage for decades of resistance, oppression, and a protracted struggle for independence.

Abandonment of the UN Plan

In 1952, the United Nations' plan to grant Eritrea autonomy and eventual independence was abandoned, leading to the federation of Eritrea with Ethiopia. Emperor Haile Selassie, motivated by territorial ambitions and strategic interests, orchestrated the annexation, dismissing the aspirations of Eritreans for self-determination. This marked a betrayal of the promises made to the Eritrean people and set the stage for a turbulent era.

Suppression of Eritrean Identity

The annexation brought about a systematic suppression of Eritrean identity. The Ethiopian government imposed Amharic as the official language, marginalized Eritrean languages, and initiated policies aimed at assimilating Eritreans into the Ethiopian cultural and political framework. This deliberate erasure of Eritrean identity fueled resentment and resistance.

Economic Exploitation and Land Redistribution

Eritrea, once boasting economic potential and infrastructure development, became a victim of economic exploitation. Resources were redirected towards Ethiopia, leaving Eritrea economically marginalized. Land redistribution policies further exacerbated tensions, as traditional Eritrean communities faced displacement and dispossession.

Emergence of Armed Resistance

As the Ethiopian government tightened its grip on Eritrea, dissent and resistance began to brew. The Eritrean Liberation Movement emerged in the late 1950s, marking the inception of armed resistance against Ethiopian rule. The struggle for self-determination gained momentum, with Eritreans from diverse backgrounds joining the fight for their rights.

The Eritrean People's Liberation Front (EPLF)

Out of the various resistance movements, the Eritrean People's Liberation Front (EPLF) emerged as a central force in the struggle for independence. Led by committed revolutionaries, the EPLF adopted a multifaceted approach, combining military prowess with social and economic development initiatives. The mountainous terrain of Eritrea became the battleground for a protracted and arduous war.

Human Cost of Resistance

The human cost of the resistance was staggering. The Ethiopian government, employing brutal tactics, engaged in widespread human rights abuses, including extrajudicial killings, torture, and mass displacement. Eritreans faced unimaginable hardships as they fought for their right to self-determination, with the struggle taking a toll on both civilians and combatants.

International Apathy and Silence

The international community largely remained indifferent to the plight of Eritreans during this period. Despite the blatant violations of human rights and the Ethiopian government's oppressive measures, global powers showed a reluctance to intervene, leaving Eritrea to endure its painful chapter of annexation largely in isolation.

Legacy and Lessons

The painful chapter of Ethiopian annexation left a lasting legacy on Eritrea. The scars of economic exploitation, cultural suppression, and human rights abuses fueled a determination among Eritreans to reclaim their sovereignty. The lessons learned from this era would shape the nation's identity, resilience, and commitment to the ideals of self-determination.

As we reflect on the painful chapter of Ethiopian annexation, it becomes clear that this period laid the foundation for the resilience and unity that define contemporary Eritrea. The struggle against annexation would become an integral part of the narrative as Eritreans forged ahead in their quest for a better future.

Armed Struggle: The Birth of the EPLF

The 1960s and 1970s witnessed the birth of a formidable force in Eritrea's struggle for independence—the Eritrean People's Liberation Front (EPLF). Emerging in response to the annexation by Ethiopia and the suppression of Eritrean identity, the EPLF became a pivotal player in the armed resistance, shaping the trajectory of the struggle and laying the groundwork for Eritrea's eventual independence.

Seeds of Resistance

The seeds of armed resistance were sown in the late 1950s as Eritreans, disillusioned by the abandonment of the United Nations' plan for self-determination, began organizing against Ethiopian rule. Various movements, including the Eritrean Liberation Movement, set the stage for a more coordinated and determined resistance that would coalesce into the EPLF.

Formation and Ideological Foundation

In 1970, the EPLF was formally established, bringing together different factions under a unified umbrella. The organization, guided by a Marxist-Leninist ideology, sought not only to liberate Eritrea from Ethiopian rule but also to address social and economic inequalities within Eritrean society. The armed struggle was thus framed within a broader context of social transformation and justice.

Military Strategy and Guerrilla Warfare

The EPLF adopted a sophisticated military strategy that blended conventional warfare with guerrilla tactics. The mountainous terrain of Eritrea became a natural fortress for the EPLF, enabling them to wage a protracted and resilient resistance against the Ethiopian military. Mobile warfare, hit-and-run tactics, and an intimate knowledge of the land became hallmarks of the EPLF's military approach.

Social and Economic Initiatives

While engaged in armed struggle, the EPLF recognized the importance of winning the hearts and minds of the Eritrean people. Social and economic initiatives were launched in the liberated areas, including the establishment of schools, healthcare facilities, and cooperatives. This dual focus on military and civilian efforts contributed to the EPLF's popularity among the Eritrean population.

International Solidarity

The EPLF actively sought international support for its cause. Solidarity campaigns were organized, drawing attention to the plight of Eritreans and garnering support from individuals, organizations, and even governments sympathetic to the struggle for self-determination. The global awareness and advocacy efforts strengthened the EPLF's position on the international stage.

Red Star Campaign

One of the iconic symbols of the EPLF's struggle was the "Red Star" campaign. The red star, prominently displayed on the EPLF flag, became a symbol of resistance and liberation. It rallied Eritreans and conveyed a message of unity and determination to the world, encapsulating the spirit of the armed struggle.

Liberation of Asmara

The culmination of the armed struggle came in 1991 with the liberation of Asmara, the capital of Eritrea. The EPLF's forces marched triumphantly into the city, marking a turning point in Eritrea's history. The liberation of Asmara not only symbolized the defeat of Ethiopian forces but also signaled the impending realization of Eritrea's long-cherished dream of independence.

Legacy and Nation-Building

The EPLF's role in the armed struggle left an indelible mark on Eritrea's identity. The resilience, sacrifice, and determination exhibited during those years became foundational elements of the nation's ethos. As Eritrea transitioned to independence in 1993, the EPLF played a central role in the early years of nation-building, shaping policies and institutions that reflected its revolutionary ideals.

The birth of the EPLF marked a crucial chapter in Eritrea's struggle for independence, embodying the spirit of resistance against external oppression and the pursuit of social justice. The organization's legacy, both in military achievements and nation-building endeavors, continues to resonate in the collective memory of Eritreans as they navigate the complexities of the present and strive for a better future.

Independence: A Hard-Fought Victory

The dawn of May 24, 1991, marked a historic moment for Eritrea—a moment decades in the making. The capital city of Asmara witnessed the triumphant entry of the Eritrean People's Liberation Front (EPLF), signaling the end of a protracted struggle for independence against Ethiopian rule. The road to sovereignty was paved with sacrifice, resilience, and unwavering determination, culminating in the realization of Eritrea's long-cherished dream.

Liberation of Asmara

The liberation of Asmara, Eritrea's capital, on May 24, 1991, marked a turning point in the struggle for independence. After years of guerrilla warfare and sacrifice, the EPLF forces, led by committed revolutionaries, marched triumphantly into the city. Asmara, once a symbol of Italian colonial rule and later Ethiopian oppression, became the symbolic heart of a free and sovereign Eritrea.

End of Ethiopian Occupation

The liberation of Asmara not only signaled the end of Ethiopian occupation but also marked the collapse of the Derg regime in Ethiopia. The fall of Mengistu Haile Mariam's government created an opportunity for Eritrea to assert its independence and embark on a new chapter in its history.

Referendum for Independence

In 1993, Eritreans exercised their right to self-determination through a UN-monitored referendum. An overwhelming 99.8% of voters chose independence, confirming the aspirations of a people who had endured decades of struggle. On April 27, 1993, Eritrea officially declared its independence, restoring its status as a sovereign nation.

Nation-Building and Reconstruction

The post-independence period was characterized by the arduous task of nation-building. The Eritrean government, initially led by the EPLF, faced the challenges of rebuilding a nation scarred by war and occupation. Efforts were directed towards reconstructing infrastructure, establishing governmental institutions, and laying the foundations for a self-reliant and prosperous future.

Social and Economic Challenges

While independence brought about a sense of national pride and sovereignty, Eritrea faced numerous social and economic challenges. The impact of the long war for independence, coupled with the need to address the aftermath of occupation, presented complex hurdles that required resilience, strategic planning, and international collaboration.

Border Conflict with Ethiopia

The euphoria of independence was, however, marred by a border conflict with Ethiopia in 1998. Disputes over the delineation of the border led to a war that lasted until 2000, resulting in significant human and economic costs for both nations. The conflict strained regional dynamics and left a lasting impact on Eritrea's geopolitical landscape.

Authoritarian Governance

The years following independence witnessed the consolidation of power under the leadership of President Isaias Afwerki. The government's approach to governance raised concerns about political freedoms, human rights, and the overall democratic trajectory of the nation. Eritrea's political landscape became a subject of international scrutiny, affecting diplomatic relations and the country's global standing.

Diaspora Contributions

The Eritrean diaspora, a significant force throughout the struggle for independence, continued to play a crucial role in the post-independence era. Contributions from Eritreans abroad, both in terms of financial remittances and advocacy efforts, became instrumental in supporting the nation's development and addressing challenges.

Resilience as a Guiding Principle

As Eritrea navigated the complexities of post-independence realities, the guiding principle remained resilience. The spirit of the Eritrean people, forged in the crucible of struggle, resilience, and sacrifice, became a driving force in confronting challenges and shaping the nation's trajectory.

The journey to independence was indeed a hard-fought victory for Eritrea, marked by triumphs, challenges, and the enduring spirit of a people determined to forge their destiny. As the nation grappled with the complexities of post-independence governance and development, the legacy of the struggle for sovereignty continued to shape Eritrea's identity and aspirations for the future.

Border Conflict with Ethiopia: A Fragile Peace

The period from 1998 to 2000 marked a tumultuous chapter in the post-independence history of Eritrea—the border conflict with Ethiopia. What began as a dispute over territory escalated into a full-scale war, resulting in significant human and economic costs for both nations. The conflict left an indelible impact on the geopolitical landscape of the region and tested the resilience of Eritrea as it navigated the complexities of a fragile peace.

Origins of the Conflict

The border conflict had its roots in the unresolved border demarcation between Eritrea and Ethiopia. Tensions mounted over the delineation of the border, particularly in the Badme region, leading to a series of skirmishes that culminated in full-scale hostilities in May 1998. The conflict quickly escalated, drawing in large military forces from both sides.

Human and Economic Toll

The war exacted a heavy toll on both Eritrea and Ethiopia. Thousands of lives were lost, and many more were displaced. The conflict disrupted economic activities, strained resources, and left a lasting impact on the social fabric of both nations. The scars of war, both physical and psychological, would be felt for years to come.

International Mediation and Peace Agreements

International efforts were undertaken to bring an end to the hostilities. The Organization of African Unity (OAU), now the African Union, played a mediation role, and various peace agreements were brokered. The Algiers Agreement of 2000, facilitated by the international community, outlined a framework for the resolution of the conflict, including the establishment of the Eritrea-Ethiopia Boundary Commission (EEBC) to demarcate the border.

Implementation Challenges

Despite the signing of the Algiers Agreement and the establishment of the EEBC, the implementation of the demarcation process faced significant challenges. Disputes over interpretation and compliance with the ruling led to a prolonged and complex stalemate. The failure to demarcate the border and implement the agreements left a lingering source of tension between Eritrea and Ethiopia.

Impact on Regional Dynamics

The border conflict had far-reaching implications for regional dynamics. It strained relationships between Eritrea and neighboring countries, influencing diplomatic ties and regional alliances. The unresolved border issue became a point of contention, affecting Eritrea's position in the Horn of Africa and contributing to a complex geopolitical landscape.

Legacy of the Conflict

The legacy of the Eritrea-Ethiopia border conflict continues to shape the political and diplomatic landscape of the region. While the Algiers Agreement established a framework for peace, the unresolved border issue remains a source of tension. The conflict also had implications for Eritrea's internal dynamics, contributing to a focus on national security and influencing governance structures.

Fragile Peace and Ongoing Challenges

The signing of the peace agreement between Eritrea and Ethiopia in July 2018 marked a significant development, leading to the normalization of diplomatic relations and the reopening of borders. However, the peace remains fragile, and the full normalization of relations faces ongoing challenges. The legacy of the conflict casts a shadow on regional dynamics, requiring sustained efforts for lasting stability.

Eritrea's Quest for Stability

As Eritrea navigates the complexities of a fragile peace, the nation remains steadfast in its quest for stability and development. The experiences of the border conflict underscore the importance of regional cooperation, diplomatic engagement, and international support in addressing the challenges and building a future marked by lasting peace and prosperity.

Authoritarian Governance: A Struggle for Democracy

In the aftermath of independence, Eritrea faced a complex political landscape marked by the consolidation of power under President Isaias Afwerki. The ideals of self-determination and the quest for a democratic system of governance that had fueled the struggle for independence encountered challenges as Eritrea grappled with an authoritarian regime. The struggle for democracy became a defining feature of the nation's post-independence era, shaping both domestic dynamics and international perceptions.

Consolidation of Power

In the years following independence, President Isaias Afwerki's government consolidated power, with the ruling People's Front for Democracy and Justice (PFDJ) becoming the dominant political force. While the Eritrean constitution, ratified in 1997, outlined democratic principles, the implementation of these principles faced challenges as political pluralism and opposition parties were marginalized.

Suppression of Dissent

A climate of political repression emerged, characterized by the suppression of dissent, restrictions on freedom of expression, and limited political freedoms. Independent media outlets were shuttered, and political opposition figures faced imprisonment. The narrowing space for civil society and political discourse became a source of concern for those advocating for democratic ideals.

National Service and Human Rights Concerns

The government's policies, particularly the indefinite national service requirement, became a focal point of international criticism and human rights concerns. National service, initially instituted for defense purposes, evolved into a system criticized for its indefinite duration, harsh conditions, and alleged human rights abuses. The impact on individual freedoms and the overall societal fabric became a central issue in discussions about Eritrea's governance.

Diaspora Activism

Eritreans in the diaspora, fueled by a commitment to democratic values and concerns for the well-being of their compatriots, became active advocates for political change. Diaspora activism took various forms, including advocacy for human rights, calls for democratic reforms, and efforts to raise awareness about the situation in Eritrea on the international stage.

International Scrutiny

The political situation in Eritrea drew international scrutiny, with human rights organizations, advocacy groups, and the United

Nations expressing concerns about governance, human rights, and political freedoms. The dynamics of Eritrea's relationship with the international community were influenced by these concerns, impacting diplomatic relations and perceptions of the nation on the global stage.

Ongoing Struggle for Democracy

The struggle for democracy in Eritrea remains an ongoing and complex process. While the government has taken steps to address some of the concerns raised by the international community, significant challenges persist. Calls for political pluralism, the rule of law, and respect for human rights continue to resonate within Eritrea and among its diaspora.

Aspirations for a Democratic Future

Despite the challenges, there are aspirations for a democratic future in Eritrea. Civil society organizations, both within the country and in the diaspora, continue to advocate for political reforms, inclusive governance, and respect for fundamental rights. The quest for democracy remains intertwined with the broader narrative of Eritrea's journey, as the nation seeks to reconcile its revolutionary ideals with the imperatives of democratic governance.

As Eritrea navigates the complexities of governance and grapples with the tension between revolutionary ideals and democratic principles, the struggle for democracy stands as a dynamic and evolving aspect of the nation's narrative. The aspirations for political pluralism, human rights, and accountable governance continue to shape the discourse about Eritrea's future.

Chapter Three

Governance Systems and Economic Struggles

The Complex Tapestry of Governance

As Eritrea emerged from the crucible of the armed struggle for independence, the challenge of crafting a governance system that aligned with the ideals of the struggle became paramount. The post-independence era saw the establishment of the People's Front for Democracy and Justice (PFDJ) as the dominant political force, consolidating power under the leadership of President Isaias Afwerki. The governance landscape, however, became a tapestry woven with complexities, marked by the tension between revolutionary ideals and the realities of political power.

The PFDJ and Political Dominance

The PFDJ, born out of the Eritrean People's Liberation Front (EPLF), emerged as the ruling party, and its influence extended across various spheres of Eritrean society. The vision of a united and self-reliant nation, central to the

EPLF's revolutionary ideals, became a guiding principle. However, concerns about political pluralism, freedom of expression, and human rights emerged as the PFDJ consolidated its political dominance.

Authoritarian Governance and Its Impact

The governance system in Eritrea took on an authoritarian character, with the concentration of power in the hands of the president and the ruling party. This approach, while rooted in the desire for stability and nation-building, faced criticism for its impact on political freedoms, civil society, and the overall democratic trajectory of the nation.

Economic Challenges and Self-Reliance

Economic struggles became intertwined with governance challenges as Eritrea sought to build a self-reliant and resilient economy. The impact of the national service requirement, initiated for defense purposes, extended to the economic sphere, influencing labor dynamics, resource allocation, and overall economic development.

Economic Struggles and Development Dilemmas

National Service and Economic Implications

The national service requirement, initially instituted to defend the nation, became a pivotal factor in shaping the economic landscape. The indefinite duration of national service led to concerns about its impact on the workforce, entrepreneurship, and the overall economic productivity of the nation.

Development Initiatives and Self-Reliance

In the pursuit of self-reliance, the Eritrean government initiated various development projects aimed at infrastructure, education, and healthcare. The emphasis on domestic resources and self-sufficiency, while aligned with the revolutionary ethos, faced challenges in the context of a changing global economic landscape.

Impact on Agriculture and Industry

Agriculture, a cornerstone of Eritrea's economy, faced challenges related to land redistribution policies and the impact of national service on the agricultural workforce. Industrial development initiatives aimed at promoting self-reliance encountered hurdles, with external factors influencing the nation's economic trajectory.

Global Context and Economic Realities

Eritrea's economic struggles occurred within the context of a globalized world, with implications for trade, investment, and development. The nation grappled with the complexities of balancing self-reliance with the need for international collaboration, facing both opportunities and challenges in the global economic arena.

Aspirations for a Sustainable Future

As Eritrea navigated the intricacies of governance and economic development, aspirations for a sustainable future remained at the forefront. The tension between revolutionary ideals, the imperatives of governance, and the complexities of economic struggles created a narrative that reflected the multifaceted nature of the nation's journey.

Voices of Change and Reform

Within Eritrea and among the diaspora, voices advocating for political reform, economic openness, and human rights gained prominence. These voices, fueled by a commitment to the nation's well-being, became integral to the ongoing dialogue about the path forward.

Challenges and Opportunities

The challenges faced by Eritrea in the realms of governance and economics were met with resilience, determination, and a commitment to national unity. While acknowledging the complexities of the journey, there remained a collective vision of overcoming challenges and harnessing opportunities for the betterment of Eritrea and its people.

Toward a Dynamic Future

Chapter 3 encapsulates the intricate interplay between governance systems and economic struggles in Eritrea's post-independence narrative. As the nation grapples with the complexities of its political and economic realities, the dynamic nature of its journey unfolds, shaped by the aspirations for a future marked by stability, prosperity, and a continued commitment to the principles that defined the struggle for independence.

The PFDJ and Political Dominance

In the aftermath of Eritrea's hard-fought independence, the political landscape was shaped by the emergence of the People's Front for Democracy and Justice (PFDJ) as the dominant political force. Born out of the revolutionary fervor of the Eritrean People's Liberation Front (EPLF), the PFDJ played a central role in steering the nation through the complexities of post-independence governance. However, this political dominance brought with it a set of challenges, raising questions about political pluralism, freedom of expression, and the overall trajectory of Eritrea's democratic ideals.

Origins and Evolution

The PFDJ traces its roots back to the EPLF, the liberation movement that spearheaded Eritrea's struggle for independence. Established officially as a political party in 1994, the PFDJ inherited the mantle of leadership, with

President Isaias Afwerki at its helm. While initially grounded in the ideals of self-determination, unity, and nation-building, the evolution of the PFDJ raised concerns about the concentration of power within the party.

Single-Party System

The PFDJ's dominance translated into a de facto single-party system in Eritrea. Political pluralism faced limitations, and opposition parties were marginalized, leading to a lack of competitive political discourse. The absence of a multi-party system raised questions about the inclusivity of governance and the representation of diverse political voices.

Suppression of Dissent

The political dominance of the PFDJ was accompanied by a climate of political repression. Dissent and opposition to the ruling party were met with harsh measures, including restrictions on freedom of expression, imprisonment of political activists, and the closure of independent media outlets. This suppression of dissent became a point of contention both domestically and internationally.

Challenges to Democratic Principles

The consolidation of power within the PFDJ posed challenges to the democratic principles that had fueled the struggle for independence. The vision of a democratic and participatory political system faced hurdles, with the ruling party's control extending to various facets of governance, including the judiciary, legislature, and executive branches.

National Service and Political Dynamics

The political dynamics within the PFDJ were intertwined with the issue of national service. The indefinite duration of national service, initially instituted for defense purposes, became a source of contention, influencing both political and economic landscapes. The impact of national service on the political dynamics within the PFDJ raised questions about governance, human rights, and the balance between security imperatives and democratic principles.

Diaspora Dissent and International Scrutiny

Eritrea's political dynamics drew attention from the international community and the Eritrean diaspora. Voices of dissent within the diaspora actively advocated for political change, human rights, and democratic reforms. International scrutiny, including reports from human rights organizations and discussions within international forums, contributed to the global discourse on Eritrea's political landscape.

Aspirations for Political Reform

Despite the challenges associated with the PFDJ's political dominance, there remained aspirations for political reform within Eritrea. Both within the country and among the diaspora, calls for increased political pluralism, the protection of human rights, and a more inclusive governance structure gained momentum.

Balancing Stability and Democratic Ideals

The question of political dominance within the PFDJ represents a delicate balance between the imperatives of stability and the aspirations for democratic ideals. As Eritrea navigates its political landscape, the challenges associated with the concentration of power underscore the complexities of aligning revolutionary principles with the evolving dynamics of democratic governance. The ongoing dialogue about political reform reflects a collective vision for a future that harmonizes stability with the democratic aspirations that have been at the heart of Eritrea's historical journey.

Authoritarian Governance and Its Impact

In the post-independence era, Eritrea has grappled with a governance system that exhibits characteristics of authoritarianism. The concentration of power within the ruling People's Front for Democracy and Justice (PFDJ) under President Isaias Afwerki's leadership has had profound implications for political freedoms, civil society, and the overall democratic trajectory of the nation. The impact of authoritarian governance in Eritrea is multifaceted, influencing various aspects of the country's political, social, and economic dynamics.

1. Suppression of Dissent:

Authoritarian governance in Eritrea has been characterized by the suppression of dissent. Political opposition figures, activists, and journalists critical of the government have faced imprisonment, leading to a climate of fear and self-censorship. The limited space for political pluralism and freedom of expression has raised concerns about the openness of political discourse.

2. Media Restrictions:

The government's control over the media landscape has been a hallmark of authoritarian governance. Independent media outlets were closed, leaving the state-controlled media as the primary source of information. This centralized control over information dissemination has limited the diversity of perspectives available to the public.

3. Constraints on Civil Society:

Authoritarian governance in Eritrea has constrained the development of a vibrant civil society. Non-governmental organizations (NGOs) face restrictions, limiting their ability to operate independently and address social issues. The suppression of civil society organizations has had implications for advocacy, human rights, and community development.

4. Political Monopoly:

The dominance of the PFDJ and the absence of a multi-party system have contributed to a political monopoly. The concentration of power within a single political entity has raised concerns about checks and balances, political competition, and the representation of diverse political voices within the governance framework.

5. National Service and Labor Dynamics:

The national service requirement, initially instituted for defense purposes, has extended to the economic sphere, impacting labor dynamics. The indefinite duration of national service has raised human rights concerns and influenced the availability of a skilled and motivated workforce for economic development.

6. Challenges to Democratic Transition:

Authoritarian governance has presented challenges to the realization of a democratic transition in Eritrea. The lack of political pluralism and the concentration of power have been identified as impediments to a more open and inclusive political system. The tension between the government's approach to governance and democratic ideals has shaped the nation's political trajectory.

7. Global Perception and Relations:

Eritrea's authoritarian governance has affected its global perception and diplomatic relations. Concerns about human rights, political freedoms, and the overall governance framework have influenced international scrutiny and diplomatic engagements. The nation's standing in the global community has been shaped by these governance dynamics.

8. Diaspora Activism:

The impact of authoritarian governance is not confined to the borders of Eritrea. Eritreans in the diaspora have become active advocates for political change, human rights, and democratic reforms. Diaspora activism reflects a commitment to the well-being of the nation and a desire to see governance that aligns with democratic principles.

9. Economic Implications:

The authoritarian governance model has implications for economic development. The concentration of political power may influence resource allocation, economic policies, and the overall business environment. Balancing the imperatives of political stability with the need for economic growth becomes a complex challenge.

10. Aspirations for Change:

Despite the challenges associated with authoritarian governance, there are aspirations for change within Eritrea. Calls for political reform, increased political pluralism, and the protection of human rights reflect a collective vision for a governance system that aligns with democratic ideals.

In navigating the impact of authoritarian governance, Eritrea faces a dynamic and evolving set of challenges and opportunities. The ongoing discourse about governance reflects a collective aspiration for a future that harmonizes political stability with the democratic principles that have been central to Eritrea's historical journey.

Economic Challenges and Self-Reliance

Eritrea's post-independence economic journey has been marked by a commitment to self-reliance, a vision rooted in the ideals of the liberation struggle. However, this pursuit of economic independence has encountered various challenges, shaping the nation's economic landscape and development trajectory.

1. National Service and Labor Dynamics:

The indefinite duration of national service, initially established for defense purposes, has had significant implications for Eritrea's labor dynamics. The conscription of a substantial portion of the population into national service has influenced the availability of skilled labor for economic activities, impacting sectors such as agriculture, industry, and services.

2. Agricultural Challenges:

Agriculture, a cornerstone of Eritrea's economy, has faced challenges related to land redistribution policies and the impact of national service on the agricultural workforce. Ensuring food security and sustainable agricultural practices has been a priority, but achieving optimal productivity has encountered hurdles.

3. Industrial Development Initiatives:

Efforts to promote industrial development and economic diversification have been integral to the self-reliance agenda. However, the challenges of mobilizing resources, technology, and skilled labor within the constraints of a small and isolated economy have posed obstacles to the realization of industrial aspirations.

4. Global Economic Context:

Eritrea's pursuit of self-reliance occurs within the broader context of a globalized economy. The challenges of attracting foreign investment, accessing international markets, and navigating global economic trends have tested the feasibility of a self-reliant economic model in an interconnected world.

5. Resource Allocation and Prioritization:

The government's approach to resource allocation and prioritization has played a crucial role in shaping the economic landscape. Balancing the imperatives of national defense, infrastructure development, and social services within the framework of self-reliance requires strategic decision-making.

6. Development Initiatives and Human Capital:

Development initiatives in education, healthcare, and infrastructure have aimed at building human capital and laying the foundations for sustainable growth. However, ensuring that these initiatives translate into a skilled and motivated workforce capable of driving economic development remains a challenge.

7. Impact of Global Crises:

Eritrea, like many nations, has been vulnerable to the impact of global economic crises. External shocks, such as fluctuations in commodity prices and disruptions in international trade, have influenced the economic stability and growth prospects of the nation.

8. Entrepreneurship and Private Sector:

Fostering entrepreneurship and a vibrant private sector is key to achieving self-reliance. Encouraging small and medium-sized enterprises (SMEs), removing bureaucratic hurdles, and creating an enabling environment for private sector growth are essential components of the economic strategy.

9. International Assistance and Aid:

While Eritrea emphasizes self-reliance, international assistance and aid have played a role in supporting development initiatives. Navigating the balance between self-reliance and external assistance involves strategic considerations and diplomatic engagement.

10. Vision for Sustainable Development:

As Eritrea grapples with economic challenges, there is a collective vision for sustainable development that balances the pursuit of self-reliance with the need for global collaboration. A strategic and adaptive approach is essential to overcoming obstacles and building a resilient and prosperous economy.

In the face of economic challenges, Eritrea's commitment to self-reliance remains central to its development narrative. The nation's ability to navigate these challenges, foster innovation, and adapt to evolving economic dynamics will shape its journey toward a sustainable and self-reliant future.

Economic Struggles and Development Dilemmas

Eritrea's post-independence journey has been characterized by economic struggles and the complexities of navigating development dilemmas. The pursuit of self-reliance, a central tenet of the nation's vision, has encountered dilemmas and challenges that have shaped the economic landscape in multifaceted ways.

1. Self-Reliance and Global Interconnectedness:

The commitment to self-reliance has been juxtaposed with the realities of a globalized world. Balancing the imperative of economic independence with the need to engage in international trade, attract foreign investment, and navigate global economic trends presents a delicate dilemma.

2. Impact of National Service on Economic Productivity:

The prolonged national service requirement, initially instituted for defense purposes, has raised dilemmas concerning its impact on economic productivity. The conscription of a significant portion of the population has implications for labor dynamics, entrepreneurship, and overall economic efficiency.

3. Industrialization and Resource Constraints:

The push for industrialization as a means of economic diversification faces dilemmas related to resource constraints. Mobilizing the necessary resources, technology, and skilled labor within the limitations of a small and isolated economy presents challenges to the realization of industrial aspirations.

4. Allocation of Resources and Prioritization:

The allocation of resources and the prioritization of development initiatives pose dilemmas for policymakers. Balancing the imperatives of national defense, infrastructure development, social services, and economic diversification requires strategic decision-making amid competing demands.

5. Global Economic Fluctuations:

Eritrea's vulnerability to global economic fluctuations introduces a dilemma in achieving economic stability. External factors, such as fluctuations in commodity prices and disruptions in international trade, can have profound implications for the nation's economic prospects.

6. Human Capital Development and Economic Growth:

The investment in human capital through education, healthcare, and infrastructure initiatives is crucial for economic growth. However, transforming these investments into a skilled and motivated workforce capable of driving economic development poses dilemmas related to skill gaps and workforce optimization.

7. Entrepreneurship and Private Sector Growth:

Fostering entrepreneurship and private sector growth is essential for economic vitality. However, dilemmas arise in creating an enabling environment for the private sector while ensuring that economic policies align with the principles of self-reliance and national development goals.

8. Strategic Use of International Assistance:

The strategic use of international assistance and aid introduces dilemmas in the pursuit of self-reliance. Navigating the balance between leveraging external support for specific development projects and maintaining sovereignty and independence requires careful diplomatic considerations.

9. Sustainable Development and Environmental Considerations:

The quest for sustainable development brings forth dilemmas related to environmental considerations. Balancing economic development with environmental preservation requires strategic planning to mitigate the impact of industrialization and infrastructure projects on ecosystems.

10. Adaptive Economic Strategies:
Eritrea's economic struggles necessitate adaptive strategies to address evolving challenges. The dilemmas faced in economic development underscore the need for flexibility, innovation, and the ability to adjust strategies based on changing circumstances.

As Eritrea grapples with economic struggles and development dilemmas, the nation's ability to navigate these complexities will be crucial for achieving sustainable and inclusive growth. The ongoing dialogue about the strategic direction of the economy reflects a collective effort to address dilemmas and build a resilient and prosperous future.

Development Initiatives and Self-Reliance

In the wake of independence, Eritrea embarked on a journey marked by development initiatives aimed at fostering self-reliance, a vision deeply rooted in the ideals of the liberation struggle.

These initiatives spanned various sectors, reflecting a commitment to nation-building and sustainable development while navigating the challenges inherent in achieving economic independence.

1. Education for Empowerment:

Development initiatives in education have been instrumental in building human capital and empowering the population. Investments in schools, vocational training centers, and higher education institutions reflect a commitment to equipping Eritreans with the skills and knowledge necessary for self-reliance.

2. Healthcare Access and Well-Being:

The provision of accessible healthcare has been a cornerstone of development initiatives. Establishing health clinics, hospitals, and preventative care programs underscores a commitment to the well-being of the population, contributing to a healthy and productive workforce.

3. Infrastructure Development:

Infrastructure projects, including roads, bridges, and energy facilities, have played a pivotal role in connecting communities and fostering economic development. Strategic investments in infrastructure contribute to self-reliance by improving connectivity and facilitating the movement of goods and people.

4. Agricultural Sustainability:

Initiatives in the agricultural sector focus on promoting sustainable practices and enhancing food security. Land redistribution policies, irrigation projects, and support for smallholder farmers aim to strengthen the agricultural foundation, reducing reliance on external sources for food.

5. Industrialization for Economic Diversification:

The push for industrialization is central to economic diversification and self-reliance. Development initiatives in manufacturing, processing, and technology aim to create a robust industrial sector capable of meeting domestic needs and generating revenue through exports.

6. Water Resource Management:

Given the arid climate in parts of Eritrea, water resource management initiatives have been crucial. Investments in water infrastructure, conservation projects, and sustainable water use practices contribute to self-reliance by ensuring a stable water supply for agricultural and domestic needs.

7. Renewable Energy Projects:

Development initiatives in renewable energy underscore a commitment to sustainability and self-sufficiency. Projects focused on harnessing solar and wind energy contribute to reducing dependency on traditional energy sources, aligning with the principles of self-reliance.

8. Entrepreneurship and Small Businesses:

Supporting entrepreneurship and small businesses is vital for economic vitality. Initiatives that provide training, access to credit, and a conducive business environment empower individuals to contribute to economic development, fostering a spirit of self-reliance.

9. Social Welfare Programs:

Social welfare programs, including poverty alleviation initiatives and support for vulnerable populations, demonstrate a commitment to inclusive development. These programs aim to create a more equitable society, where all citizens can actively participate in and benefit from the nation's progress.

10. Strategic Diplomacy for Economic Collaboration:

Engaging in strategic diplomacy to foster economic collaboration with regional and international partners is part of Eritrea's self-reliance strategy. Bilateral and multilateral partnerships can contribute to technology transfer, investment, and knowledge exchange, strengthening the nation's economic resilience.

11. Agricultural Cooperatives and Community Development:

Initiatives that promote agricultural cooperatives and community-based development empower local communities. By fostering self-sufficiency at the grassroots level, these initiatives contribute to the overarching goal of national self-reliance.

As Eritrea pursues development initiatives, the goal of achieving self-reliance remains at the forefront of the nation's narrative. These initiatives, spanning various sectors, reflect a comprehensive strategy aimed at building a resilient and sustainable economy that can thrive independently in the global community. The ongoing commitment to self-reliance positions Eritrea on a path of inclusive development and collective prosperity.

Impact on Agriculture and Industry

Eritrea's journey toward self-reliance and sustainable development has significantly shaped the agricultural and industrial sectors. The impact of development initiatives, economic policies, and external factors has influenced the dynamics of these crucial components of the nation's economy.

1. Agriculture:

Land Redistribution Policies:

Eritrea's land redistribution policies, aimed at achieving equitable access to and utilization of arable land, have had a transformative impact on agriculture. By redistributing land to smallholder farmers, the government seeks to enhance productivity and reduce dependency on traditional farming practices.

Irrigation and Water Management:

Initiatives focused on irrigation and water resource management aim to address the challenges posed by Eritrea's arid climate. Sustainable water use practices and infrastructure development contribute to increased agricultural yields, promoting food security and self-sufficiency.

Impact of National Service:

The impact of the prolonged national service requirement on the agricultural workforce has been a notable factor. While national service was initially instituted for defense purposes, its influence on labor dynamics in agriculture has prompted discussions about optimizing workforce availability for economic productivity.

Challenges and Opportunities:

Despite progress, challenges such as climate variability and limited access to modern agricultural technologies persist. Innovations in sustainable farming practices, coupled with community-based initiatives, offer opportunities to address these challenges and strengthen the agricultural sector.

2. Industry:

Industrialization and Economic Diversification:

Eritrea's push for industrialization is a key component of its economic diversification strategy. Development initiatives in manufacturing, processing, and technology aim to reduce dependency on traditional sectors, creating opportunities for value addition and revenue generation.

Resource Constraints:

The industrial sector grapples with resource constraints inherent in a small and isolated economy. Mobilizing resources, including skilled labor and technology, poses challenges to the realization of industrial aspirations, necessitating strategic planning and adaptive approaches.

Global Economic Context:

Eritrea's industrialization efforts occur within the context of a globalized economy. The nation faces the dilemma of balancing self-reliance with the need for international collaboration, trade, and investment to support industrial growth and competitiveness.

Entrepreneurship and Small Businesses:

Supporting entrepreneurship and small businesses is crucial for the vibrancy of the industrial sector. Initiatives that provide training, access to credit, and a conducive business environment empower individuals to contribute to economic development and foster a diverse industrial landscape.

Sustainable Practices:

Industrial development initiatives increasingly emphasize sustainable practices to minimize environmental impact. Balancing economic growth with environmental considerations is integral to the nation's commitment to responsible and sustainable industrialization.

3. Synergies and Interconnectedness:

Integrated Development Approach:

The impact on agriculture and industry reflects the interconnectedness of these sectors within Eritrea's development narrative. An integrated approach, where the agricultural and industrial sectors complement each other, is essential for achieving self-reliance and sustainable economic growth.

Community-Based Development:

Community-based development initiatives, encompassing both agriculture and industry, empower local communities to actively participate in and benefit from the nation's progress. Strengthening these grassroots initiatives contributes to a more inclusive and resilient national development framework.

Diplomatic Collaboration for Industrial Growth:

Engaging in strategic diplomacy to foster economic collaboration and technology transfer is pivotal for industrial growth. Bilateral and multilateral partnerships can enhance the industrial sector's capabilities, contributing to economic resilience and self-reliance.

In navigating the impact on agriculture and industry, Eritrea faces a dynamic and evolving landscape. The nation's commitment to sustainable practices, strategic planning, and a comprehensive approach to development positions it on a path toward economic resilience and self-sufficiency. Balancing the challenges and opportunities within the agricultural and industrial sectors is integral to realizing the vision of a self-reliant and prosperous Eritrea.

Global Context and Economic Realities

Eritrea's economic trajectory unfolds within the broader context of a globalized world, where interconnectedness, trade dynamics, and geopolitical factors shape the nation's economic realities. Navigating the challenges and opportunities presented by the global context is integral to Eritrea's pursuit of self-reliance and sustainable development.

1. Trade and International Collaboration:

Eritrea's economic landscape is influenced by its engagement in international trade and collaboration. The nation seeks to leverage diplomatic relations and trade partnerships to access markets, attract foreign investment, and foster technology transfer. Strategic collaborations contribute to economic diversification and resilience.

2. Foreign Direct Investment (FDI):

The global context plays a crucial role in Eritrea's ability to attract foreign direct investment. The nation's investment climate, diplomatic relations, and economic policies influence the decisions of foreign investors. Balancing the imperatives of economic openness with the principles of self-reliance is a delicate consideration.

3. Commodity Prices and Economic Stability:

Eritrea's economy is sensitive to fluctuations in global commodity prices. The nation's reliance on certain exports makes it susceptible to market dynamics. Economic stability is influenced by the ability to adapt to price changes and diversify revenue sources, reducing vulnerability to external shocks.

4. Global Economic Crises:

The occurrence of global economic crises can impact Eritrea's economic stability. External factors, such as recessions and financial downturns, pose challenges to growth and development. The nation's ability to navigate these crises requires adaptive economic strategies and a resilient financial framework.

5. Technological Advancements and Innovation:

The rapid pace of technological advancements globally presents both challenges and opportunities for Eritrea. Embracing innovation is crucial for enhancing productivity, improving competitiveness, and fostering economic growth. Access to and adoption of new technologies contribute to the nation's resilience in the face of global changes.

6. Climate Change and Environmental Considerations:

The global discourse on climate change has implications for Eritrea's economic realities. Environmental considerations, including sustainable practices and climate-resilient strategies, are integral to the nation's commitment to responsible development.

Adaptation to changing environmental conditions is a key aspect of economic planning.

7. Multilateral Organizations and Development Assistance:

Eritrea engages with multilateral organizations to access development assistance, technical expertise, and collaborative initiatives. Diplomatic efforts and partnerships with international organizations contribute to the nation's development agenda, providing avenues for knowledge exchange and support.

8. Global Market Access:

Access to global markets is essential for Eritrea's economic growth. Trade agreements, market diversification, and compliance with international standards enhance the nation's ability to participate in the global economy. Ensuring competitiveness in the global marketplace is a strategic consideration.

9. Diaspora Contributions and Remittances:

Eritrea's diaspora plays a significant role in the nation's economic realities. Remittances from

Eritreans living abroad contribute to the country's foreign exchange reserves and support the well-being of families. Harnessing the potential of the diaspora for investment and knowledge transfer is part of the economic strategy.

10. Global Health Crises and Resilience:
Global health crises, as demonstrated by events such as pandemics, impact economic and social structures. Building resilience in healthcare systems, adopting proactive measures, and ensuring adaptability to global health challenges are essential components of Eritrea's economic planning.

In navigating the global context and economic realities, Eritrea faces the challenge of balancing its pursuit of self-reliance with the need for international collaboration. Strategic diplomacy, adaptive economic strategies, and a comprehensive understanding of global dynamics are integral to the nation's journey toward economic resilience and sustainable development. The ongoing dialogue with the global community shapes Eritrea's position in the complex and interconnected world of the 21st century.

Aspirations for a Sustainable Future

As Eritrea navigates the complexities of governance, economic development, and global dynamics, the aspirations for a sustainable future remain at the forefront of the nation's narrative. The collective vision encompasses multifaceted dimensions, reflecting the aspirations of the people, the challenges faced, and the principles that underpin Eritrea's historical journey.

1. Democracy and Political Pluralism:

Eritrea aspires to foster a political landscape characterized by democracy, political pluralism, and active citizen participation. The vision includes the establishment of inclusive governance structures that respect human rights, uphold the rule of law, and provide avenues for diverse voices to contribute to the nation's development.

2. Economic Resilience and Diversification:

The pursuit of economic resilience involves a commitment to diversification and self-reliance. Eritrea aspires to build a diverse and robust economy, capable of withstanding external shocks and adapting to global economic changes. Economic initiatives aim to create opportunities for innovation, entrepreneurship, and sustainable development.

3. Social Inclusion and Welfare:

The vision for a sustainable future in Eritrea prioritizes social inclusion and welfare. The nation aspires to build a society where all citizens have equal opportunities for education, healthcare, and social services. Community-based initiatives and social welfare programs contribute to a more equitable and inclusive society.

4. Environmental Sustainability:

Eritrea's commitment to a sustainable future includes proactive measures for environmental preservation. Aspirations involve adopting eco-friendly practices, mitigating the impact of climate change, and balancing economic development with environmental conservation.

Responsible natural resource management is a key component of this vision.

5. Global Collaboration and Diplomacy:

Eritrea aspires to play a constructive role in the global community through diplomatic engagements and collaborations. The vision includes building positive relations with neighboring countries, participating in international forums, and contributing to global initiatives for peace, security, and sustainable development.

6. Harnessing Technology for Development:

Embracing technological advancements is part of Eritrea's vision for a sustainable future. The nation aspires to harness the power of innovation and technology to enhance productivity, improve education and healthcare, and foster economic growth. Bridging the digital divide and investing in research and development are integral to this aspiration.

7. Youth Empowerment and Education:

The future sustainability of Eritrea rests on empowering the youth through education and skill development. Aspirations include providing quality education, vocational training, and opportunities for youth entrepreneurship. A well-educated and skilled workforce is seen as vital for the nation's progress.

8. Cultural Preservation and Identity:

Eritrea aspires to preserve and celebrate its rich cultural heritage and identity. The vision includes initiatives to safeguard cultural traditions, languages, and historical landmarks. Cultural preservation is viewed as essential for fostering a sense of national pride and unity.

9. Community-Based Development Initiatives:

A sustainable future in Eritrea involves empowering local communities through community-based development initiatives. Aspirations include supporting cooperatives, small businesses, and grassroots projects that enhance self-sufficiency and contribute to the overall development of the nation.

10. Responsive Healthcare System:

The vision for a sustainable future includes the establishment of a responsive and accessible healthcare system. Aspirations involve improving healthcare infrastructure, addressing public health challenges, and ensuring that citizens have access to quality healthcare services.

11. Adaptive Governance and Democratic Reforms:

Eritrea aspires to adopt adaptive governance structures that respond to the evolving needs of its citizens. Democratic reforms, transparency, and the protection of human rights are integral to the vision. The nation seeks to build institutions that reflect the principles of democracy and good governance.

As Eritrea envisions a sustainable future, the journey involves navigating challenges, harnessing opportunities, and staying true to the principles that have defined the nation's historical narrative. The aspirations reflect a commitment to resilience, inclusivity, and the well-being of the people, paving the way for a future marked by stability, prosperity, and sustainable development.

Voices of Change and Reform

In Eritrea, amidst the complexities of governance, economic challenges, and global dynamics, a chorus of voices advocating for change and reform has emerged. These voices, emanating from within the nation and its diaspora, reflect a collective desire for transformation and progress. The diverse array of perspectives and narratives underscores the dynamic dialogue surrounding the future of Eritrea.

1. Diaspora Advocacy:

Eritreans in the diaspora have become influential voices calling for change and reform. Activists, intellectuals, and community leaders in the diaspora actively engage in advocacy efforts, raising awareness about human rights issues, governance concerns, and the need for democratic reforms within Eritrea.

2. Youth Engagement:

The youth of Eritrea, both within the country and abroad, represent a powerful force advocating for change. Social media platforms, artistic expressions, and grassroots movements have become channels for the youth to voice their aspirations for political openness, economic opportunities, and a more inclusive society.

3. Intellectual Discourse:

Within academic and intellectual circles, there is a vibrant discourse on the future of Eritrea. Scholars, researchers, and thought leaders contribute to the dialogue, offering insights on governance models, economic strategies, and pathways to sustainable development. Their perspectives influence the broader narrative of change.

4. Civil Society Activism:

Civil society organizations within Eritrea and in the diaspora play a crucial role in advocating for change. These organizations focus on human rights, democracy, and social justice. Their efforts include documenting human rights violations, engaging with international bodies, and fostering community-based initiatives.

5. Media and Journalism:

Independent media outlets, although limited, serve as platforms for voices advocating change. Journalists and media professionals, often working under challenging conditions, contribute to transparency and accountability by reporting on governance issues, human rights concerns, and societal challenges.

6. Political Dissent:

Despite restrictions on political opposition within Eritrea, there are individuals and groups advocating for political pluralism and democratic reforms. These voices, often facing significant risks, call for an inclusive political landscape that embraces diverse perspectives and fosters a participatory democracy.

7. Community-Based Initiatives:

At the community level, there are grassroots initiatives promoting positive change. Community leaders, religious figures, and local activists engage in projects that address social issues, support vulnerable populations, and contribute to the overall well-being of communities.

8. International Advocacy:

International human rights organizations, advocacy groups, and diplomatic entities contribute to the voices calling for change in Eritrea. Reports, campaigns, and diplomatic efforts aim to shed light on human rights abuses, advocate for political reforms, and engage with the Eritrean government on issues of concern.

9. Economic Visionaries:

Voices advocating for economic reform and innovation are prominent within discussions about Eritrea's future. Economic visionaries propose strategies for sustainable development, job creation, and economic diversification, emphasizing the importance of harnessing technology and engaging in global markets.

10. Collaboration for Change:

Calls for collaboration, both within Eritrea and with the international community, echo through the voices of change and reform. The emphasis is on dialogue, cooperation, and collective efforts to address challenges, foster development, and build a more inclusive and prosperous future.

While the voices of change and reform in Eritrea represent diverse perspectives and visions, they collectively contribute to a dynamic dialogue about the nation's future. The ongoing discourse reflects a shared aspiration for positive transformation, emphasizing principles of democracy, human rights, and sustainable development.

Challenges and Opportunities on the Path to Progress

As Eritrea navigates its journey toward progress and sustainable development, a landscape of challenges and opportunities unfolds. Acknowledging and addressing these elements is crucial for crafting effective strategies that lead to positive transformation. The intricate interplay between challenges to overcome and opportunities to seize shapes the narrative of Eritrea's ongoing development.

Challenges:

Authoritarian Governance: The enduring challenge of authoritarian governance poses obstacles to political openness, pluralism, and citizen participation. Addressing this challenge requires navigating the complexities of political reform and building institutions that uphold democratic principles.

Human Rights Concerns: Persistent human rights concerns, including limitations on freedom of expression and arbitrary detentions, present challenges to creating an environment that respects and protects the rights of individuals. Achieving progress involves addressing these issues through legal reforms and institutional changes.

Economic Sustainability: The pursuit of economic sustainability faces challenges such as resource constraints, global economic fluctuations, and the impact of national service on labor dynamics. Balancing the imperatives of economic growth with self-reliance requires strategic planning and adaptive economic strategies.

Global Economic Integration: While global economic integration presents opportunities, it also brings challenges related to market competitiveness, trade dynamics, and attracting foreign investment. Navigating these challenges involves positioning Eritrea strategically in the global marketplace.

Climate Change and Environmental Impact: The impact of climate change poses challenges to agricultural productivity and environmental sustainability. Developing resilience strategies, implementing sustainable practices, and addressing water scarcity are imperative for mitigating the environmental impact.

Healthcare Infrastructure: Strengthening healthcare infrastructure remains a challenge, particularly in the context of global health crises. Building a responsive and robust healthcare system requires investments in infrastructure, healthcare personnel, and strategies for disease prevention and control.

Youth Unemployment: Addressing youth unemployment is a pressing challenge that requires targeted strategies for skill development, job creation, and entrepreneurship. Engaging the youth in the economic and social fabric of the nation is essential for sustainable development.

Access to Information: Limited access to independent information and media restrictions pose challenges to transparency and accountability. Fostering an environment where diverse voices can be heard and informed discussions can take place is crucial for societal progress.

Opportunities:

Diaspora Engagement: The Eritrean diaspora presents a significant opportunity for engagement, collaboration, and resource mobilization. Leveraging the skills, expertise, and networks of the diaspora can contribute to economic development, knowledge transfer, and advocacy for positive change.

Human Capital Development: Investing in human capital through education, vocational training, and healthcare initiatives provides an opportunity to build a skilled and motivated workforce. A well-educated population is an asset for economic growth and sustainable development.

Community-Based Initiatives: Community-based initiatives, driven by local leaders and activists, offer opportunities for addressing social challenges at the grassroots level. Empowering communities to take an active role in their development contributes to a more inclusive and resilient society.

Technological Innovation: Embracing technological innovation presents opportunities for economic diversification, improved productivity, and global competitiveness. Harnessing the power of technology can transform key sectors and contribute to Eritrea's economic resilience.

Global Partnerships: Building strategic partnerships with regional and international entities opens avenues for collaboration, trade, and development assistance. Engaging with the global community fosters diplomatic relations and supports initiatives for economic growth.

Natural Resource Management: Strategic natural resource management, including sustainable agriculture and responsible mining practices, provides opportunities for economic development while mitigating environmental impact. Balancing economic activities with environmental conservation is essential.

Cultural Heritage and Tourism: Eritrea's rich cultural heritage and historical landmarks present opportunities for tourism development. Promoting cultural preservation and sustainable tourism practices can contribute to economic growth and global recognition.

Youth Entrepreneurship: Encouraging youth entrepreneurship through initiatives that provide training, access to credit, and a conducive business environment can address youth unemployment and contribute to economic vitality.

Civil Society Engagement: Strengthening civil society organizations and supporting their advocacy efforts provides an avenue for promoting transparency, human rights, and democratic values. An active civil society contributes to the checks and balances within the governance framework.

Strategic Diplomacy: Engaging in strategic diplomacy fosters opportunities for collaboration, foreign investment, and international support. Building positive diplomatic relations contributes to Eritrea's standing in the global community.

As Eritrea grapples with challenges and seizes opportunities, the nation stands at a critical juncture in its pursuit of progress. Crafting inclusive and adaptive strategies, fostering a spirit of innovation, and embracing constructive dialogue can pave the way for a future marked by resilience, prosperity, and sustainable development.

Challenges and Opportunities on the Path to Progress

Eritrea faces a complex landscape of challenges and opportunities as it strives for progress and sustainable development. Identifying and addressing these elements is essential for crafting effective strategies that lead to positive transformation. The interplay between challenges to overcome and opportunities to seize shapes the narrative of Eritrea's ongoing development.

Challenges:

Authoritarian Governance: The persistent challenge of authoritarian governance poses obstacles to political openness, pluralism, and citizen participation. Addressing this challenge requires navigating the complexities of political reform and building institutions that uphold democratic principles.

Human Rights Concerns: Ongoing human rights concerns, including limitations on freedom of expression and arbitrary detentions, present challenges to creating an environment that respects and protects individual rights. Achieving progress involves addressing these issues through legal reforms and institutional changes.

Economic Sustainability: The pursuit of economic sustainability faces challenges such as resource constraints, global economic fluctuations, and the impact of national service on labor dynamics. Balancing the imperatives of economic growth with self-reliance requires strategic planning and adaptive economic strategies.

Global Economic Integration: While global economic integration presents opportunities, it also brings challenges related to market competitiveness, trade dynamics, and attracting foreign investment. Navigating these challenges involves positioning Eritrea strategically in the global marketplace.

Climate Change and Environmental Impact: The impact of climate change poses challenges to agricultural productivity and environmental sustainability. Developing resilience strategies, implementing sustainable practices, and addressing water scarcity are imperative for mitigating the environmental impact.

Healthcare Infrastructure: Strengthening healthcare infrastructure remains a challenge, particularly in the context of global health crises. Building a responsive and robust healthcare system requires investments in infrastructure, healthcare personnel, and strategies for disease prevention and control.

Youth Unemployment: Addressing youth unemployment is a pressing challenge that requires targeted strategies for skill development, job creation, and entrepreneurship. Engaging the youth in the economic and social fabric of the nation is essential for sustainable development.

Access to Information: Limited access to independent information and media restrictions pose challenges to transparency and accountability. Fostering an environment where diverse voices can be heard and informed discussions can take place is crucial for societal progress.

Opportunities:

Diaspora Engagement: The Eritrean diaspora presents a significant opportunity for engagement, collaboration, and resource mobilization. Leveraging the skills, expertise, and networks of the diaspora can contribute to economic development, knowledge transfer, and advocacy for positive change.

Human Capital Development: Investing in human capital through education, vocational training, and healthcare initiatives provides an opportunity to build a skilled and motivated workforce. A well-educated population is an asset for economic growth and sustainable development.

Community-Based Initiatives: Community-based initiatives, driven by local leaders and activists, offer opportunities for addressing social challenges at the grassroots level. Empowering communities to take an active role in their development contributes to a more inclusive and resilient society.

Technological Innovation: Embracing technological innovation presents opportunities for economic diversification, improved productivity, and global competitiveness. Harnessing the power of technology can transform key sectors and contribute to Eritrea's economic resilience.

Global Partnerships: Building strategic partnerships with regional and international entities opens avenues for collaboration, trade, and development assistance. Engaging with the global community fosters diplomatic relations and supports initiatives for economic growth.

Natural Resource Management: Strategic natural resource management, including sustainable agriculture and responsible mining practices, provides opportunities for economic development while mitigating environmental impact. Balancing economic activities with environmental conservation is essential.

Cultural Heritage and Tourism: Eritrea's rich cultural heritage and historical landmarks present opportunities for tourism development. Promoting cultural preservation and sustainable tourism practices can contribute to economic growth and global recognition.

Youth Entrepreneurship: Encouraging youth entrepreneurship through initiatives that provide training, access to credit, and a conducive business environment can address youth unemployment and contribute to economic vitality.

Civil Society Engagement: Strengthening civil society organizations and supporting their advocacy efforts provides an avenue for promoting transparency, human rights, and democratic values. An active civil society contributes to the checks and balances within the governance framework.

Strategic Diplomacy: Engaging in strategic diplomacy fosters opportunities for collaboration, foreign investment, and international support. Building positive diplomatic relations contributes to Eritrea's standing in the global community.

As Eritrea grapples with challenges and seizes opportunities, the nation stands at a critical juncture in its pursuit of progress. Crafting inclusive and adaptive strategies, fostering a spirit of innovation, and embracing constructive dialogue can pave the way for a future marked by resilience, prosperity, and sustainable development.

Toward a Dynamic Future: Navigating Challenges and Embracing Opportunities

Eritrea stands at a pivotal juncture on its journey toward a dynamic and sustainable future. Acknowledging the challenges that lie ahead and embracing the array of opportunities can shape the nation's narrative of progress. In the spirit of resilience, innovation, and inclusivity, Eritrea can chart a course toward a future marked by prosperity, democratic values, and global collaboration.

1. Political Evolution and Democratic Reforms:

Embracing a political evolution that prioritizes democratic values is fundamental for Eritrea's dynamic future. Initiating and sustaining democratic reforms can lead to inclusive governance structures, increased citizen participation, and the protection of human rights.

2. Empowering the Youth:

The youth represent the driving force behind Eritrea's dynamic future. Investing in education, skill development, and entrepreneurship creates opportunities for the youth to contribute actively to economic growth and social development.

3. Economic Diversification and Innovation:

Economic sustainability hinges on diversification and innovation. Encouraging technological advancements, supporting small businesses, and fostering an environment that stimulates entrepreneurship can propel Eritrea toward a more vibrant and dynamic economy.

4. Global Collaboration and Diplomacy:

Strategic diplomacy and active engagement with the global community open doors for collaboration, foreign investment, and knowledge exchange. Building positive diplomatic relations positions Eritrea as a dynamic player on the international stage.

5. Environmental Stewardship:

Prioritizing sustainable practices and environmental stewardship is crucial for long-term resilience. Investing in renewable energy, responsible resource management, and climate adaptation strategies ensures a dynamic future that respects the delicate balance between development and environmental preservation.

6. Inclusive Healthcare and Social Services:

Strengthening healthcare infrastructure and social services contributes to a resilient and healthy population. Prioritizing inclusivity in access to quality healthcare and social programs fosters a society that cares for its citizens.

7. Technology for Development:

Embracing technological advancements and digital innovation enhances productivity and competitiveness. Harnessing technology for education, healthcare, and economic development positions Eritrea on the forefront of the global digital landscape.

8. Cultural Preservation and Tourism:

Valuing and preserving cultural heritage not only fosters national pride but also presents opportunities for tourism. Sustainable tourism initiatives can showcase Eritrea's rich history and contribute to economic growth.

9. Community-Led Development Initiatives:

Empowering local communities through community-led initiatives ensures that development is inclusive and responsive to diverse needs. Supporting grassroots projects fosters a sense of ownership and collective responsibility.

10. Youth Engagement in Governance:
Actively involving the youth in governance structures and decision-making processes ensures a dynamic and representative leadership. Youth engagement fosters fresh perspectives, innovation, and a deeper connection between the government and the aspirations of the population.

11. Investment in Education and Research:

A commitment to education and research creates a knowledge-based society. Investing in academic institutions, research facilities, and intellectual pursuits contributes to a dynamic future built on a foundation of continuous learning and innovation.

12. Transparent Governance and Accountability: Fostering transparency, accountability, and the rule of law strengthens the foundations of good governance. Implementing mechanisms for accountability ensures that the government remains responsive to the needs and aspirations of the people.

As Eritrea strides toward a dynamic future, the convergence of political will, societal engagement, and strategic planning will be crucial. By addressing challenges with resilience and seizing opportunities with innovation, Eritrea can craft a narrative of progress that resonates both nationally and globally. The vision for a dynamic future is a collective endeavor, shaped by the aspirations and contributions of the Eritrean people.

Chapter Four

Eritrean Diaspora

A Tapestry of Global Voices

The Eritrean diaspora, scattered across continents, is a vibrant and diverse community that weaves a tapestry of global voices deeply connected to the homeland. This chapter delves into the multifaceted nature of the Eritrean diaspora, exploring its formation, the challenges faced by its members, and the profound impact it has on both the individuals within it and the development of Eritrea itself.

1. *Origins and Dynamics*

1.1 Historical Migration Waves:

The Eritrean diaspora is shaped by historical migration waves, with roots tracing back to Italian colonization, the struggle for independence, and subsequent geopolitical developments. Understanding these historical contexts provides insight into the diverse backgrounds and experiences of Eritreans abroad.

1.2 Forced Migration and Refugee Experiences:

The diaspora includes those who fled Eritrea due to conflict, political persecution, or economic hardships. Exploring the stories of forced migration and refugee experiences sheds light on the challenges faced by Eritreans seeking safety and stability in foreign lands.

2. *Challenges Faced by the Diaspora*

2.1 Identity and Cultural Preservation:

Maintaining a strong connection to Eritrean identity and culture while living in diverse and often assimilative societies presents a challenge for the diaspora. The chapter explores how Eritreans abroad navigate the delicate balance between assimilation and cultural preservation.

2.2 Political Divisions and Activism:

The diaspora is not immune to the political divisions that exist within Eritrea. The chapter delves into how these divisions manifest among diaspora communities and explores the role of activism in advocating for political change and human rights.

2.3 Socioeconomic Integration and Struggles:

Eritreans abroad face the challenges of socioeconomic integration, including issues related to education, employment, and discrimination. Examining these struggles provides insights into the resilience of the diaspora and the efforts made to overcome barriers.

3. *Impact on Families and Homeland*

3.1 Remittances and Economic Support:

Remittances from the diaspora play a crucial role in supporting families in Eritrea. The chapter analyzes the economic impact of remittances on individual households and explores how this financial lifeline shapes the economic landscape of the homeland.

3.2 Transnational Identities and Connections:

The transnational identities formed by Eritreans abroad and their ongoing connections to the homeland are explored. The chapter examines how technology, including social media, facilitates communication, activism, and the maintenance of familial and cultural ties across borders.

4. *Community Engagement and Initiatives*

4.1 Diaspora Organizations and Networks:

Diaspora organizations and networks play a pivotal role in fostering community engagement. The chapter highlights the diverse organizations, from cultural associations to human rights groups, that contribute to the collective voice and agency of the Eritrean diaspora.

4.2 Philanthropy and Development Initiatives:

Examining philanthropic efforts and development initiatives led by the diaspora provides insight into the broader impact beyond individual remittances. The chapter explores projects aimed at education, healthcare, and infrastructure development in Eritrea.

5. *Diaspora Perspectives on Eritrea's Future*

5.1 Aspirations for Change:

The diaspora is a reservoir of aspirations for change and reform in Eritrea. This section explores the diverse perspectives within the diaspora regarding the future of the homeland, encompassing visions for political openness, human rights, and sustainable development.

5.2 Challenges in Advocacy:

Advocacy for change faces challenges within the diaspora, including differing political views, generational gaps, and the complexities of engaging with a homeland under authoritarian governance. The chapter navigates these challenges and explores how the diaspora contributes to the broader discourse on Eritrea's future.

6. *Conclusion: Building Bridges for a Collective Future*

6.1 Unity in Diversity:

Despite the challenges faced by the diaspora, the chapter concludes by emphasizing the unity in diversity that characterizes Eritrean communities worldwide. It explores the potential of the diaspora to serve as a bridge for dialogue, understanding, and collaboration, contributing to a collective vision for a dynamic and prosperous future for Eritrea.

Historical Migration Waves:

The Eritrean diaspora traces its origins to historical migration waves deeply intertwined with the nation's complex past. Understanding these waves provides a foundational insight into the diverse backgrounds and experiences of Eritreans abroad.

Colonial Legacy:

The first wave of Eritrean migration can be traced back to the Italian colonial era, where the convergence of cultures and labor needs led to the movement of Eritreans within and beyond the region. The legacies of this period continue to shape the cultural fabric of the diaspora, as families established roots in various corners of the world.

Struggle for Independence:

The subsequent significant wave of migration occurred during the protracted struggle for Eritrea's independence from Ethiopian rule. Eritreans fled the conflict, seeking refuge in neighboring countries and distant lands. This period saw the formation of the diaspora as a result of both forced displacement and voluntary migration driven by the desire to contribute to the cause of liberation.

Post-Independence Era:

Following Eritrea's hard-fought independence in 1991, a wave of hope and optimism spurred voluntary migration. Many Eritreans abroad returned to contribute to the nation's rebuilding process. However, political developments and the challenges of nation-building prompted a subsequent wave of migration, with individuals leaving in search of better economic opportunities and political freedoms.

Impact on Cultural Identity:

These historical migration waves have left an indelible mark on the cultural identity of the diaspora. The experiences of displacement, resilience, and the pursuit of self-determination are woven into the narratives of Eritreans living abroad. As they carry the echoes of their history, the diaspora becomes a repository of diverse cultural expressions, preserving traditions, languages, and customs.

Generational Perspectives:

Each migration wave has engendered distinct generational perspectives within the diaspora. Older generations often carry memories of the struggle for independence and the challenges of displacement. Younger generations, born or raised abroad, navigate the complexities of dual identities, seeking to reconcile their Eritrean heritage with the cultural influences of their adopted countries.

Cultural Diaspora Centers:

Cities such as London, Washington D.C., Rome, and Toronto have emerged as cultural diaspora centers, where Eritrean communities gather, celebrate their heritage, and grapple with the complexities of preserving cultural identity in diverse societies. These centers serve as hubs for social cohesion, cultural exchange, and collective efforts to address shared challenges.

Impact on Advocacy and Activism:

The historical migration waves have not only shaped the diaspora's identity but also fueled its activism. Eritreans abroad, spurred by a sense of duty and shared history, engage in advocacy for human rights, political reform, and social justice. The diaspora's collective voice reverberates globally, amplifying its call for a better future for Eritrea.

In exploring the historical migration waves, this section sets the stage for a deeper understanding of the Eritrean diaspora's evolution and its intricate connections to the homeland. The subsequent sections will delve into the challenges faced by the diaspora, its impact on families and the homeland, and the diverse initiatives and perspectives that characterize this global community.

Forced Migration and Refugee Experiences:

The Eritrean diaspora is profoundly influenced by forced migration and refugee experiences, reflecting the challenging historical periods that compelled individuals to seek safety and stability in foreign lands. This section delves into the narratives of Eritreans who faced displacement due to conflict, political persecution, and economic hardships.

The Exodus during Conflict:

One significant wave of forced migration occurred during periods of conflict, including the Eritrean War of Independence (1961-1991) and the subsequent Eritrean-Ethiopian War (1998-2000). As conflict escalated, Eritreans faced difficult choices, with many compelled to flee their homes to escape violence, persecution, and the impact of war on their communities.

Refugees in Neighboring Countries:

Eritreans sought refuge in neighboring countries, including Sudan and Ethiopia, where refugee camps became temporary homes for those escaping conflict. These camps, though providing a semblance of safety, were marked by challenging conditions, limited resources, and the uncertainty of the future.

Dangers of Irregular Migration:

Forced migration also led to the perilous journeys of Eritreans attempting to cross borders in search of safety. The dangers of irregular migration, including human trafficking, exploitation, and perilous desert and sea crossings, became harsh realities for those compelled to flee their homeland.

Impact on Families and Communities:

Forced migration fractured families and communities, separating loved ones and dispersing them across different regions and continents. The trauma of displacement and the challenges of rebuilding lives in unfamiliar environments left indelible marks on the psyche of those who experienced forced migration.

Asylum-Seekers and Legal Challenges:

Eritreans seeking asylum faced legal challenges in host countries. Navigating complex asylum processes, language barriers, and adapting to new legal systems became part of the refugee experience. Despite the challenges, many Eritreans persevered, determined to secure a stable and secure future for themselves and their families.

Integration and Resilience:

As refugees resettled in various parts of the world, they encountered the challenges of integration into new societies. Language barriers, cultural differences, and the need to establish new livelihoods tested their resilience. Overcoming these challenges, Eritreans in the diaspora forged new lives while retaining a deep connection to their homeland.

Humanitarian Response and International Support:

International humanitarian organizations played a crucial role in responding to the needs of Eritrean refugees. The provision of aid, educational opportunities, and healthcare services in refugee camps contributed to sustaining the displaced population during times of uncertainty.

Generational Impact:

The forced migration experiences had a generational impact, shaping the identity and outlook of those born or raised outside Eritrea. The younger generation in the diaspora, often referred to as the "children of exile," navigates the complexities of dual identities and grapples with the challenges of preserving cultural heritage in foreign environments.

Advocacy for Refugees and Human Rights:

The forced migration experiences have fueled advocacy efforts within the Eritrean diaspora.

Many individuals and organizations actively engage in advocating for the rights of refugees, drawing attention to the plight of those who have faced forced migration and the need for international support.

In exploring forced migration and refugee experiences, this section sheds light on the resilience of Eritreans who, in the face of adversity, sought refuge in foreign lands. The subsequent sections will delve into the challenges faced by the diaspora, its impact on families and the homeland, and the diverse initiatives and perspectives that characterize this global community.

2. Challenges Faced by the Diaspora

2.1 Identity and Cultural Preservation:

The Eritrean diaspora faces the ongoing challenge of preserving its identity and cultural heritage while navigating diverse and often assimilative societies. This section explores the multifaceted dimensions of identity and the efforts made by Eritreans abroad to maintain a strong connection to their roots.

Navigating Dual Identities:

Eritreans in the diaspora often find themselves navigating dual identities. Born or raised in countries with distinct cultural norms, languages, and traditions, they grapple with the balancing act of preserving their Eritrean identity while embracing aspects of their adopted culture. This dual identity is a dynamic and evolving aspect of the diaspora experience.

Language Preservation:

Language is a cornerstone of cultural identity, and the diaspora faces the challenge of preserving Eritrean languages, including Tigrinya, Tigre, and Arabic, in environments where the dominant language may be different. Language schools, community programs, and digital platforms become crucial in maintaining linguistic ties to Eritrea.

Cultural Practices and Traditions:

Preserving cultural practices and traditions requires intentional efforts within diaspora communities. From traditional dances and ceremonies to culinary traditions, Eritreans abroad actively engage in cultural events, community gatherings, and initiatives that celebrate and pass down their rich heritage to younger generations.

Generational Shifts:

Generational shifts within the diaspora present a unique challenge. The younger generation, often born or raised outside Eritrea, may have distinct perspectives on cultural identity. Balancing the expectations of older generations with the evolving cultural expressions of the youth becomes a delicate intergenerational dialogue.

Religious Practices:

Religious diversity is a hallmark of the Eritrean diaspora, with followers of Christianity and Islam coexisting within communities. Preserving religious practices and fostering mutual respect among diverse religious backgrounds contribute to the cultural tapestry of the diaspora.

Community Cohesion:

Building and maintaining a cohesive Eritrean community in the diaspora is essential for cultural preservation. Community organizations, cultural associations, and religious institutions serve as focal points for fostering a sense of belonging and providing platforms for cultural expression.

Challenges of Assimilation:

While embracing the diversity of their adopted countries, Eritreans in the diaspora face the challenge of assimilation. Striking a balance between integration into the broader society and preserving distinct cultural identities requires navigating social, educational, and workplace environments.

Media and Digital Influence:

The influence of media and digital platforms poses both opportunities and challenges. While these mediums provide a connection to Eritrean news, entertainment, and cultural content, they also expose the diaspora to global trends that may impact traditional cultural practices.

Role of Educational Initiatives:

Educational initiatives within diaspora communities play a vital role in cultural preservation. Eritrean schools, cultural exchange programs, and mentorship initiatives contribute to the transmission of cultural knowledge and values across generations.

Celebrating Diversity within the Diaspora:

Acknowledging and celebrating the diversity within the diaspora itself is crucial. Different regions, migration waves, and cultural influences contribute to a rich mosaic of identities. Embracing this diversity fosters a sense of unity while appreciating the unique contributions of each subgroup.

Preserving identity and cultural heritage is an ongoing journey for the Eritrean diaspora. By actively engaging in cultural initiatives, fostering intergenerational dialogue, and celebrating diversity, Eritreans abroad navigate the complexities of identity preservation while contributing to the vibrant cultural landscape of their adopted countries.

2.2 Political Divisions and Activism:

Within the Eritrean diaspora, the complexities of political divisions and activism form a significant aspect of the community's dynamics. This section delves into the diverse political perspectives among Eritreans abroad, the impact of these divisions on community cohesion, and the role of activism in advocating for political change and human rights.

Diverse Political Perspectives:

The Eritrean diaspora reflects a spectrum of political perspectives, shaped by historical events, individual experiences, and generational differences. These perspectives range from those supportive of the current government to those advocating for political reforms or change.

Impact on Community Cohesion:

Political divisions can pose challenges to community cohesion within the diaspora. Disagreements over the assessment of Eritrea's political landscape, the role of the government, and the direction for the nation's future can strain relationships and hinder collaborative efforts within the community.

Generational Differences:

Generational differences contribute to diverse political views within the diaspora. Older generations, shaped by experiences of the independence struggle, may hold different perspectives from the younger generation, born or raised in the diaspora and influenced by global political trends.

Role of Activism:

Activism within the Eritrean diaspora plays a crucial role in expressing dissent, advocating for political change, and promoting human rights. Activist groups, both online and offline, mobilize to raise awareness about issues in Eritrea, lobby for international intervention, and engage in advocacy campaigns.

Challenges of Advocacy:

Advocacy within the diaspora faces challenges, including navigating legal restrictions on activism, addressing the diversity of political opinions, and managing external influences. Balancing the pursuit of justice with maintaining community unity requires strategic and inclusive approaches.

Human Rights Advocacy:

A significant focus of diaspora activism is human rights advocacy. Eritrean activists shine a spotlight on issues such as political repression, limitations on freedom of expression, and arbitrary detentions in Eritrea. Their efforts contribute to the global discourse on human rights violations.

Diaspora Media Outlets:

Diaspora media outlets, including online platforms, play a vital role in shaping narratives and disseminating information. These outlets provide a space for diverse voices, including those critical of the government, fostering a sense of community and facilitating discussions on political developments.

International Lobbying:

Eritrean diaspora activists engage in lobbying efforts at international forums, urging governments and organizations to address human rights concerns in Eritrea. These efforts aim to garner international support for initiatives promoting political openness, justice, and respect for human rights.

Dialogue Initiatives:

Despite political divisions, some members of the diaspora actively engage in dialogue initiatives. Forums for constructive conversations allow individuals with differing political views to find common ground, fostering understanding and collaboration on issues of mutual concern.

Impact on Homeland Perception:

The political dynamics within the diaspora influence global perceptions of Eritrea. The diversity of opinions and activism contributes to a nuanced understanding of the complex political landscape, challenging monolithic narratives and emphasizing the importance of diverse perspectives.

Navigating political divisions and engaging in activism are intrinsic aspects of the Eritrean diaspora experience. As the community grapples with these complexities, the pursuit of justice, human rights, and a shared vision for Eritrea's future remains central to the diaspora's collective efforts.

2.3 Socioeconomic Integration and Struggles:

Socioeconomic integration poses significant challenges for the Eritrean diaspora as they establish new lives in diverse countries. This section explores the struggles faced by Eritreans abroad in areas such as education, employment, and the broader aspects of adapting to new economic landscapes.

Education Challenges:

Access to quality education can be a complex issue for Eritreans in the diaspora. Language barriers, differences in educational systems, and financial constraints may hinder smooth transitions into the educational systems of host countries. Educational initiatives within the diaspora seek to address these challenges and support academic success.

Employment Barriers:

Eritreans in the diaspora often face barriers in the job market, including discrimination, credential recognition issues, and challenges related to language proficiency. These barriers may contribute to underemployment or limited career advancement, prompting efforts within the community to address employment challenges.

Entrepreneurship and Business Ventures:

To overcome employment challenges, some members of the diaspora turn to entrepreneurship and business ventures. Starting businesses allows individuals to leverage their skills, contribute to the local economy, and create employment opportunities. However, entrepreneurship also comes with its own set of challenges, including access to capital and navigating regulatory environments.

Financial Strain and Remittances:

Economic struggles can lead to financial strain within the diaspora. Remittances, often sent back to support family members in Eritrea, play a significant role in mitigating financial challenges. However, the obligation to send remittances may also contribute to personal financial stress for individuals within the diaspora.

Community Support Networks:

Recognizing the challenges of socioeconomic integration, community support networks within the diaspora play a crucial role. Networking, mentorship programs, and initiatives that share information about job opportunities and educational resources help create a supportive environment for individuals navigating new economic landscapes.

Cultural Adaptation and Workplace Dynamics:

Adapting to workplace dynamics in a new cultural context can be challenging. Navigating office culture, understanding professional norms, and addressing potential biases require adaptability and resilience. Cultural competence initiatives within the diaspora aim to provide guidance on these aspects of socioeconomic integration.

Generational Perspectives on Success:

Generational perspectives within the diaspora influence perceptions of success. While older generations may prioritize stability through traditional professions, younger generations may seek success through non-traditional paths, including entrepreneurship, creative pursuits, and social impact initiatives.

Access to Social Services:

Access to social services, including healthcare, can be a concern for the diaspora. Differences in healthcare systems, insurance coverage, and navigating public services may pose challenges. Community-led initiatives often emerge to provide support and information on accessing essential social services.

Language Proficiency and Communication:

Language proficiency is a key factor in socioeconomic integration. Proficiency in the language of the host country facilitates effective communication, job opportunities, and overall integration. Language programs and community-driven language initiatives assist in addressing language barriers and enhancing communication skills.

Resilience and Collective Efforts:

Despite the challenges, resilience and collective efforts within the diaspora contribute to overcoming socioeconomic barriers.

Community-led programs, mentorship initiatives, and advocacy for equal opportunities underscore the commitment of the diaspora to creating a more inclusive and supportive environment for all its members.

Addressing the socio economic struggles of the Eritrean diaspora involves a multi-faceted approach, encompassing education, employment, financial empowerment, and community support. By navigating these challenges collectively, the diaspora works towards fostering a more equitable and prosperous future for its members.

3. Impact on Families and Homeland

3.1 Remittances and Economic Support:

One of the profound ways in which the Eritrean diaspora contributes to the well-being of their families and homeland is through remittances—financial support sent back to loved ones in Eritrea. This section explores the impact of remittances on individual households, the broader economic landscape of the homeland, and the complexities associated with this crucial lifeline.

Economic Lifeline for Families:

Remittances serve as a crucial economic lifeline for families in Eritrea. Many households depend on these financial transfers from their relatives abroad to cover basic needs such as housing, education, healthcare, and daily expenses. The consistent flow of remittances often provides a sense of stability and security for recipients.

Education and Skill Development:

A significant portion of remittances is directed towards supporting education and skill development. Families use these funds to cover school fees, purchase educational materials, and invest in skill-building initiatives. The impact of remittances on education contributes to the empowerment and future prospects of the younger generation in Eritrea.

Healthcare and Medical Expenses:

Remittances play a vital role in addressing healthcare needs and covering medical expenses. Families use these funds to access quality healthcare services, purchase medications, and navigate health challenges. The impact of remittances on health care contributes to the overall well-being of individuals and communities.

Housing and Infrastructure Development:

Remittances often contribute to housing and infrastructure development within families. They may be utilized to build or improve homes, ensuring better living conditions. Additionally, funds from remittances may be pooled for community-level projects, enhancing local infrastructure and amenities.

Entrepreneurship and Small Businesses:

Some families leverage remittances to start or expand small businesses. Whether in agriculture, trade, or services, the financial support from the diaspora can serve as seed capital for entrepreneurial endeavors. This contributes to economic diversification and community-level economic resilience.

Reduction of Poverty and Financial Vulnerability:

Remittances play a pivotal role in reducing poverty and financial vulnerability among recipient families. The steady income from abroad provides a safety net, helping families withstand economic shocks, unforeseen expenses, or fluctuations in local economic conditions.

Impact on Local Economies:

On a broader scale, the collective impact of remittances contributes to the stability of local economies. The infusion of foreign currency enhances liquidity, supports local businesses, and fuels economic activities. Remittances contribute to the overall economic resilience of communities across Eritrea.

Challenges and Complexities:

While remittances bring substantial benefits, there are challenges and complexities associated with their impact. Dependence on remittances can create a risk of complacency in local economic development, and the uneven distribution of remittances may contribute to social and economic disparities within communities.

Long-Term Development Initiatives:

Recognizing the need for sustainable development, some families invest remittance funds in long-term development initiatives. These may include projects related to agriculture, renewable energy, education infrastructure, and healthcare facilities. Such initiatives aim to foster self-reliance and contribute to the overall development of the homeland.

Emotional and Social Impact:

Beyond the economic contributions, remittances have emotional and social impacts. They strengthen family ties, foster a sense of connection between diaspora members and their homeland, and contribute to the maintenance of cultural identity across generations.

Remittances, as a powerful conduit of support, weave a thread of connectivity between the Eritrean diaspora and their families in the homeland. The sustained flow of financial assistance not only addresses immediate needs but also holds the potential to catalyze transformative change and development within Eritrea.

3.2 Transnational Identities and Connections:

The Eritrean diaspora, scattered across the globe, maintains transnational identities and connections that transcend geographic boundaries. This section explores how technology, including social media and digital communication, facilitates transnational connections, influences cultural identities, and shapes the relationships between diaspora members and their homeland.

Digital Bridges Across Borders:

In the digital age, technology serves as a powerful bridge connecting Eritreans in the diaspora with their homeland. Social media platforms, instant messaging, and video calls provide real-time communication, enabling individuals to stay connected with family, friends, and community members across continents.

Cultural Preservation through Technology:

Digital platforms play a pivotal role in preserving and promoting Eritrean culture.

From online cultural events and language learning apps to virtual celebrations of traditional festivals, technology serves as a dynamic tool for cultural exchange, ensuring that heritage is passed down to younger generations.

Virtual Communities and Support Networks:

Online forums and diaspora-specific social networks create virtual communities where Eritreans share experiences, offer support, and discuss matters related to identity, culture, and homeland affairs. These platforms foster a sense of belonging and community among diaspora members who may be geographically dispersed.

Political Activism and Awareness:

Technology amplifies the voices of Eritrean diaspora activists. Social media campaigns, online petitions, and digital advocacy efforts raise awareness about human rights abuses, political issues, and the need for democratic reforms in Eritrea. The digital sphere becomes a powerful space for shaping international discourse.

Preserving Language and Multilingualism:

Digital platforms contribute to the preservation of Eritrean languages. Language learning apps, online tutorials, and virtual language schools empower diaspora members, especially the younger generation, to maintain proficiency in Tigrinya, Tigre, and other languages, fostering multilingualism within the community.

Global Collaboration and Initiatives:

Technology facilitates global collaboration on initiatives for Eritrea's development. Diaspora members can engage in joint projects, share resources, and coordinate efforts to address challenges faced by their homeland. Virtual collaboration enhances the collective impact of diaspora-led initiatives.

Information Flow and Homeland Dynamics:

The instantaneous flow of information through digital channels shapes diaspora members' understanding of homeland dynamics. News, updates, and personal narratives shared online provide insights into the evolving socio-political landscape of Eritrea, influencing diaspora perspectives and activism.

Economic Contributions and Fintech:

Technology plays a role in facilitating economic contributions to Eritrea. Online banking, mobile money transfers, and financial technology platforms simplify the process of sending remittances, making financial support more efficient and accessible for diaspora members and their families.

Challenges of Digital Disconnect:

Despite the benefits, a digital disconnect can emerge. Not all diaspora members have equal access to technology, leading to potential disparities in information flow and participation. Addressing digital divides within the diaspora is essential to ensure inclusivity and equitable engagement.

Balancing Virtual and Physical Identities:

While technology facilitates transnational connections, diaspora members navigate the balance between virtual and physical identities. Sustaining tangible connections with the homeland, beyond the digital realm, remains crucial for maintaining a holistic sense of cultural identity and heritage.

In navigating the digital landscape, Eritreans in the diaspora actively shape and engage with transnational identities. The interplay of technology, culture, and activism creates a dynamic tapestry that connects individuals across borders and contributes to the evolving narrative of the Eritrean diaspora.

4. Community Engagement and Initiatives

4.1 Diaspora Organizations and Networks:

Community engagement within the Eritrean diaspora is fostered through a myriad of organizations and networks. This section explores the diverse range of diaspora organizations, their roles in building a sense of community, and the initiatives they undertake to address the needs of their members and contribute to the development of Eritrea.

Cultural Associations:

Cultural associations are foundational to diaspora communities, serving as hubs for preserving and promoting Eritrean heritage. These organizations organize cultural events, language classes, and traditional celebrations, providing a space for community members to connect, share experiences, and maintain a strong cultural identity.

Human Rights Advocacy Groups:

Human rights advocacy groups within the diaspora play a crucial role in raising awareness about human rights abuses in Eritrea. Through campaigns, public forums, and engagement with international organizations, these groups amplify the voices of those affected and advocate for justice, political openness, and the respect of human rights.

Religious and Faith-Based Organizations:

Religious and faith-based organizations contribute to the spiritual well-being of the diaspora. They provide spaces for worship, community support, and cultural preservation. These organizations often engage in charitable initiatives, supporting both their local communities abroad and projects in Eritrea.

Youth and Student Associations:

Youth and student associations cater to the specific needs of younger diaspora members. They organize educational events, mentorship programs, and forums for cultural exchange. These associations play a vital role in empowering the younger generation to navigate the challenges of dual identity and become active contributors to their communities.

Professional and Business Networks:

Professional and business networks within the diaspora facilitate career development, networking, and mentorship. These organizations connect professionals, entrepreneurs, and individuals in various industries, fostering collaboration and providing resources for career advancement.

Advocacy and Political Organizations:

Advocacy and political organizations focus on addressing political issues, promoting democracy, and advocating for human rights in Eritrea. Through lobbying efforts, campaigns, and engagement with international bodies, these organizations contribute to the global discourse on Eritrea's political landscape.

Educational Initiatives:

Educational initiatives within the diaspora aim to address challenges related to education and skill development. Language schools, scholarship programs, and educational resources help diaspora members, especially the younger generation, maintain a connection to their heritage while pursuing academic excellence in their host countries.

Philanthropic and Development Organizations:

Philanthropic and development organizations focus on initiatives aimed at supporting Eritrea's development. These projects may include healthcare initiatives, infrastructure development, and community-based programs. The diaspora's collective financial contributions and expertise play a crucial role in driving sustainable development in Eritrea.

Media and Communications Outlets:

Media and communications outlets within the diaspora contribute to information dissemination and community engagement. Newspapers, websites, and online platforms provide news, analysis, and cultural content, serving as vital channels for keeping diaspora members informed and connected.

Sports and Recreational Groups:

Sports and recreational groups offer a platform for community members to come together in a non-formal setting. These organizations organize sports events, tournaments, and recreational activities, fostering camaraderie and providing an avenue for physical well-being within the diaspora.

Collaboration on Global Challenges:

Diaspora organizations collaborate on addressing global challenges, such as the impact of the COVID-19 pandemic, natural disasters, or humanitarian crises. Joint efforts leverage the collective strengths of the diaspora to provide support, resources, and solidarity in times of need.

Challenges of Inclusivity and Diversity:

While diaspora organizations play a crucial role, challenges of inclusivity and diversity may arise. Efforts to ensure representation, engage diverse perspectives, and address generational differences are essential for fostering a sense of belonging and unity within the broader diaspora community.

Diaspora organizations and networks, with their diverse focuses and initiatives, form the backbone of community engagement. Through these organizations, the Eritrean diaspora actively shapes its narrative, addresses challenges, and contributes to the well-being of its members and the development of Eritrea.

5. Diaspora Perspectives on Eritrea's Future

5.1 Aspirations for Change:

The Eritrean diaspora, fueled by a deep connection to their homeland, holds diverse perspectives on the future of Eritrea. This section explores the aspirations for change within the diaspora, encompassing calls for political reform, human rights, and a vision for a more democratic and inclusive Eritrea.

Calls for Political Reform:

Many within the diaspora advocate for political reform in Eritrea, emphasizing the importance of democratic governance, political openness, and citizen participation. Calls for constitutional reforms, inclusive political dialogue, and a multi-party system reflect the aspirations for a governance structure that reflects the will of the people.

Demands for Human Rights:

Human rights advocacy is a central focus of diaspora efforts. The call for the respect of human rights in Eritrea includes demands for freedom of expression, an end to arbitrary detentions, and the release of political prisoners. The diaspora actively engages with international human rights organizations to amplify these demands on a global stage.

Vision for a Pluralistic Society:

A vision for a pluralistic and inclusive Eritrea is articulated by many in the diaspora. Embracing diversity in all its forms, including ethnic, religious, and cultural diversity, is seen as essential for building a harmonious society that values the contributions of all its members.

Empowerment of Women and Youth:

Empowering women and youth is a key aspiration within the diaspora. Calls for gender equality, increased opportunities for education and employment, and the involvement of young people in decision-making processes reflect a commitment to nurturing the potential of these demographic groups for the betterment of Eritrea.

Support for Economic Development:

Economic development features prominently in diaspora aspirations. Calls for sustainable economic policies, poverty reduction initiatives, and efforts to harness the potential of the diaspora for investments and entrepreneurship underscore the commitment to building a prosperous and self-reliant nation.

Dialogue and Reconciliation:

Many within the diaspora advocate for inclusive dialogue and reconciliation processes. Recognizing the scars of past conflicts, there is a desire for healing and unity. Initiatives that foster open conversations, address historical grievances, and promote national reconciliation are seen as crucial for Eritrea's future.

International Engagement and Collaboration:

Engaging with the international community is a shared aspiration. The diaspora seeks collaborations with international partners, governments, and organizations to address the challenges faced by Eritrea. International support is viewed as instrumental in achieving positive change and fostering a climate of cooperation.

Preservation of Cultural Heritage:

Preserving Eritrea's rich cultural heritage is a common goal within the diaspora. Efforts to promote cultural exchange, language preservation, and the celebration of traditions aim to ensure that future generations maintain a strong connection to their Eritrean identity.

Environmental Sustainability:

A commitment to environmental sustainability is articulated by some in the diaspora. As the global community grapples with environmental challenges, there is a desire to see Eritrea pursue sustainable development practices that prioritize environmental conservation and address climate-related concerns.

Inclusive Development Initiatives:

Inclusive development initiatives are advocated to ensure that the benefits of progress are shared equitably among all segments of the population. Diaspora members express a commitment to projects that address disparities, improve infrastructure, and enhance the quality of life for all Eritreans.

Participation in Homeland Affairs:

An aspiration for increased diaspora participation in homeland affairs is evident. Calls for mechanisms that allow diaspora input in decision-making processes, voting rights for Eritreans abroad, and enhanced diaspora engagement channels reflect a desire for active involvement in shaping the nation's future.

Balancing Tradition and Modernity:

Finding a balance between tradition and modernity is a nuanced aspiration. The diaspora envisions a future Eritrea that honors cultural heritage while embracing innovation and progress, fostering a society that draws strength from its roots while adapting to the challenges and opportunities of the contemporary world.

As the diaspora envisions the future of Eritrea, these aspirations reflect a collective commitment to positive change, democratic governance, and the well-being of the nation and its people. The multifaceted perspectives within the diaspora contribute to a dynamic and evolving dialogue about the path forward for Eritrea.

Chapter Five

Impact on Families and Communities

5.1 Transnational Bonds:

The Eritrean diaspora, scattered across the globe, is bound by transnational connections that traverse geographic boundaries. Families and communities maintain intricate webs of relationships that bridge continents, facilitated by advancements in technology. The impact of these transnational bonds is profound, shaping the dynamics of familial connections and community cohesion.

Virtual Reunions: Digital platforms enable virtual reunions, allowing families to connect in real-time regardless of physical distance. Video calls, instant messaging, and social media become avenues for sharing milestones, participating in celebrations, and providing emotional support.

Generational Ties: The younger generation in the diaspora maintains strong ties to Eritrea through digital communication. Virtual connections with grandparents, extended family, and community elders foster the transmission of cultural values, oral traditions, and linguistic heritage to the next generation.

Cultural Exchange: Transnational connections facilitate continuous cultural exchange. Families in the diaspora actively engage in preserving and celebrating Eritrean traditions, sharing cultural practices, and organizing virtual events that bring the richness of Eritrean heritage to the forefront.

5.2 Educational Opportunities:

The impact of the Eritrean diaspora on education is multifaceted, influencing both individuals and the broader community. Aspirations for educational excellence, language preservation, and skill development shape the educational landscape for diaspora members.

Language Preservation Initiatives: Language schools and online language programs thrive within the diaspora. These initiatives aim to preserve Eritrean languages, ensuring that younger generations maintain proficiency and a deep connection to their linguistic roots.

Educational Empowerment: The diaspora actively supports educational empowerment, providing resources for academic pursuits. Scholarships, mentorship programs, and community-led initiatives create pathways for individuals to access quality education and pursue their academic goals.

Skill Building for Empowerment: Recognizing the importance of skill development, the diaspora engages in initiatives that empower individuals with practical skills. Workshops, vocational training programs, and mentorship opportunities contribute to the professional growth and self-reliance of community members.

5.3 Economic Resilience:

Economic ties between the Eritrean diaspora and their homeland play a pivotal role in fostering resilience within families and communities. Remittances, entrepreneurial endeavors, and collaborative economic initiatives contribute to economic stability and development.

Remittances as a Lifeline: Remittances serve as a lifeline for families in Eritrea, addressing immediate needs and providing a sense of financial stability. The consistent flow of remittances contributes to poverty reduction and economic resilience within recipient households.

Entrepreneurship and Economic Diversity: Some diaspora members channel their economic contributions into entrepreneurship and business ventures. This entrepreneurial spirit not only supports individual livelihoods but also contributes to economic diversity within the community and the homeland.

Community-Led Development Projects: The diaspora engages in community-led development projects that address local needs. From healthcare initiatives to infrastructure development, collaborative efforts enhance the overall economic landscape, creating sustainable benefits for the broader community.

5.4 Challenges and Resilience:

While the impact of the Eritrean diaspora is substantial, challenges persist. Navigating generational differences, addressing disparities, and ensuring inclusive development require collective efforts. Despite challenges, the resilience of families and communities within the diaspora shines through.

Generational Dynamics: Generational differences pose challenges in maintaining cultural traditions and navigating identity. The diaspora actively engages in intergenerational dialogue, fostering understanding and unity while ensuring the transmission of cultural heritage to younger generations.

Inclusivity and Representation: Diaspora communities grapple with the need for inclusivity and representation. Efforts to address disparities, amplify diverse voices, and create platforms for meaningful participation aim to build a more inclusive community that embraces the diversity of its members.

Adaptive Strategies: In the face of challenges, families and communities within the diaspora exhibit adaptive strategies. From leveraging technology for communication to creating support networks, the diaspora actively seeks innovative solutions to overcome obstacles and foster resilience.

5.5 Cultural Renaissance:

The diaspora is a catalyst for a cultural renaissance, breathing life into Eritrean traditions, art, and expressions. Cultural associations, virtual events, and collaborative initiatives contribute to a vibrant cultural landscape that transcends physical borders.

Celebrating Heritage: Cultural associations play a central role in celebrating Eritrean heritage. Through traditional events, festivals, and cultural showcases, the diaspora ensures that the richness of Eritrean culture thrives, providing a source of pride and connection.

Artistic Expressions: Artists within the diaspora contribute to a burgeoning artistic scene. Whether through music, literature, or visual arts, the diaspora's creative expressions become a testament to the resilience, aspirations, and diverse experiences of Eritrean communities.

Preserving Oral Traditions: In a digital age, the diaspora actively engages in preserving oral traditions. Elders within the community share stories, wisdom, and historical narratives, ensuring that the oral heritage of Eritrea is passed down through generations.

5.6 Advocacy for Change:

The diaspora serves as a vocal advocate for change within Eritrea. Calls for political reform, human rights, and a vision for a more democratic and inclusive future echo through the activism and engagement of diaspora members.

Human Rights Advocacy: Human rights advocacy groups within the diaspora amplify the voices of those affected by human rights abuses in Eritrea. Through campaigns, engagement with international organizations, and awareness initiatives, the diaspora contributes to the global discourse on human rights.

Political Engagement: Political organizations within the diaspora actively engage in advocating for political change. Calls for democratic governance, constitutional reforms, and citizen participation underscore the diaspora's commitment to shaping a political landscape that reflects the aspirations of the people.

Global Collaboration: Engaging with the international community, the diaspora collaborates on global challenges. From humanitarian crises to public health emergencies, the diaspora's global networks and collaborations contribute to addressing shared challenges and fostering solidarity.

Transnational Bonds:

The Eritrean diaspora, spread across the globe, weaves a complex tapestry of transnational bonds that defy geographical distances. These bonds, nurtured by advancements in technology, redefine the nature of familial connections and community cohesion. The impact of transnational bonds is profound, influencing relationships, cultural preservation, and the overall sense of belonging among diaspora members.

Virtual Reunions:

Technology serves as a bridge, enabling families to maintain a sense of closeness despite physical separation. Video calls, instant messaging, and social media platforms facilitate virtual reunions, allowing families to share daily moments, celebrations, and important milestones in real-time. These digital connections become lifelines, fostering a continuous and intimate link between generations.

Generational Ties:

The younger generation, born or raised in the diaspora, actively maintains ties with their Eritrean roots through digital communication. Virtual connections with grandparents, aunts, uncles, and extended family members become a crucial link to cultural heritage and traditions. This intergenerational dialogue enriches the identity of younger diaspora members, creating a nuanced understanding of their Eritrean heritage.

Cultural Exchange:

Transnational bonds facilitate a vibrant exchange of culture among diaspora communities. Online platforms become stages for cultural events, language classes, and celebrations of Eritrean traditions. Whether through virtual coffee ceremonies, language learning apps, or digital storytelling, the diaspora actively engages in preserving and sharing its cultural wealth.

Support Networks:

Digital platforms create robust support networks within the diaspora. Whether in times of joy or difficulty, these networks offer emotional support, guidance, and a sense of community. Online forums and social media groups become spaces where diaspora members share advice, resources, and stories, fostering a collective strength that transcends borders.

Preservation of Language:

Language, a cornerstone of cultural identity, is actively preserved through transnational bonds. Language schools, online tutorials, and digital resources empower diaspora members, especially the younger generation, to maintain proficiency in Tigrinya, Tigre, and other languages. This commitment to linguistic heritage becomes a powerful link to the roots of Eritrean identity.

Global Celebrations:

Digital connectivity enables diaspora members to participate in global celebrations of Eritrean culture. Whether it's Independence Day, religious festivals, or traditional ceremonies, virtual participation ensures that the diaspora remains actively connected to the collective celebrations of their homeland. Live Streamed events and online gatherings create a sense of unity and shared identity.

Maintaining Traditions:

Transnational bonds play a crucial role in maintaining and adapting cultural traditions. Elders within the diaspora become storytellers, passing down oral traditions, historical narratives, and wisdom to younger generations. Virtual spaces become modern-day meeting grounds for the continuation of age-old practices, ensuring the preservation of cultural heritage.

Navigating Dual Identities:

For diaspora members, transnational bonds provide a framework for navigating dual identities. The blending of Eritrean heritage with the cultural nuances of their adopted countries becomes a dynamic process. Digital communication facilitates open conversations about identity, fostering an environment where individuals can confidently embrace the richness of their diverse backgrounds.

Emotional Resilience:

In times of political uncertainty or global challenges, transnational bonds contribute to emotional resilience. Families and communities find solace in the ability to connect, share experiences, and offer support, regardless of the physical distances that separate them. This emotional resilience becomes a testament to the strength of the diaspora's interconnectedness.

Building a Global Eritrean Community:

Transnational bonds contribute to the formation of a global Eritrean community. Beyond individual families, the diaspora becomes a collective force, united by a shared history, cultural heritage, and aspirations for the future.

Digital platforms serve as the threads weaving this global community together, creating a tapestry of connections that spans continents.

In navigating transnational bonds, the Eritrean diaspora not only maintains a strong connection to its roots but also actively contributes to the preservation and evolution of Eritrean culture. The interplay of technology, cultural exchange, and emotional support forms the foundation of a dynamic and resilient diaspora community.

Educational Opportunities:

The Eritrean diaspora places a significant emphasis on education, viewing it as a cornerstone for individual empowerment and community development. As families and communities navigate the challenges and opportunities in their adopted countries, educational initiatives within the diaspora become crucial elements in shaping a brighter future for Eritrean youth and fostering a deep connection to their cultural roots.

Language Preservation Initiatives:

Preserving Eritrean languages is a priority within the diaspora. Language schools, both physical and virtual, are established to ensure that younger generations maintain proficiency in Tigrinya, Tigre, and other languages. These initiatives go beyond linguistic skills, actively engaging students in cultural immersion and heritage preservation.

Educational Empowerment Programs:

The diaspora actively supports educational empowerment programs that provide resources for academic excellence. Scholarship initiatives, mentorship programs, and community-led efforts aim to create opportunities for Eritrean youth to pursue higher education, professional development, and skill-building.

Skill Development Workshops:

Recognizing the importance of practical skills in navigating the challenges of the diaspora experience, skill development workshops are organized. These workshops cover a range of areas, including entrepreneurship, vocational training, and technology literacy, empowering individuals to contribute to their communities and pursue diverse career paths.

Cultural Education Initiatives:

Cultural education initiatives play a vital role in shaping the identity of Eritrean youth in the diaspora. Programs that integrate cultural studies into mainstream education, virtual cultural exchanges, and extracurricular activities foster a sense of pride and connection to Eritrean heritage.

Mentorship Programs:

Mentorship programs within the diaspora provide guidance and support to young Eritreans navigating educational and career pathways. Seasoned professionals and community leaders actively engage in mentorship, sharing their experiences, insights, and expertise to empower the next generation.

Access to Higher Education:

Efforts are made to facilitate access to higher education for Eritrean youth in the diaspora. Diaspora communities collaborate with educational institutions, scholarship foundations, and governmental bodies to create pathways for young individuals to pursue academic excellence and contribute to their chosen fields.

Virtual Learning Platforms:

In an increasingly digital world, virtual learning platforms become essential tools for educational initiatives. Online courses, webinars, and digital resources enable diaspora members to access educational opportunities regardless of geographic location. These platforms contribute to the continuous learning and skill enhancement of the diaspora community.

Support for STEM Education:

Recognizing the importance of STEM (Science, Technology, Engineering, and Mathematics) education, the diaspora actively supports initiatives that encourage Eritrean youth to pursue careers in these fields. STEM-focused programs, coding workshops, and science clubs empower young minds to explore and excel in these critical areas.

Educational Partnerships:

Educational partnerships between diaspora organizations and institutions in Eritrea create collaborative opportunities. Exchange programs, research initiatives, and joint educational ventures strengthen ties between the diaspora and the homeland, fostering a sense of shared commitment to educational excellence.

Promoting Lifelong Learning:

The diaspora embraces a culture of lifelong learning, encouraging individuals to continually expand their knowledge and skills. Whether through online courses, community-led workshops, or collaborative learning initiatives, the commitment to learning becomes a shared value within the diaspora community.

Navigating Dual Educational Systems:

As diaspora youth navigate dual educational systems—balancing the expectations of their adopted countries and the cultural values of Eritrea—support systems are established. Educational counseling, cultural sensitivity training for educators, and community-led initiatives aim to create environments where individuals can thrive academically while maintaining a strong connection to their Eritrean identity.

In navigating educational opportunities, the Eritrean diaspora actively invests in the intellectual growth and cultural preservation of its youth. These initiatives contribute not only to the academic success of individuals but also to the collective strength and resilience of the diaspora community. Education becomes a powerful vehicle for empowerment, cultural continuity, and the realization of future aspirations.

Challenges and Resilience:

The journey of the Eritrean diaspora is marked by a tapestry of challenges, yet within these difficulties, families and communities demonstrate remarkable resilience. As they navigate the complexities of cultural adaptation, generational dynamics, and societal integration, the diaspora emerges stronger, weaving stories of tenacity, unity, and collective strength.

Generational Dynamics:

The diaspora grapples with generational differences as younger members, raised in a different cultural context, negotiate their Eritrean identity. Balancing the preservation of cultural heritage with the influences of their adopted countries requires open dialogues and concerted efforts to bridge generational gaps.

Inclusivity and Representation:

Ensuring inclusivity and representation within the diaspora community is an ongoing challenge. Striving to amplify diverse voices, address disparities, and create platforms for underrepresented groups become essential for fostering a sense of belonging and unity within the broader community.

Adapting to Cultural Shifts:

Cultural shifts, influenced by the diaspora experience and external societal changes, present challenges in maintaining traditional values. Families and communities engage in ongoing conversations about adapting to these shifts while preserving the core tenets of Eritrean culture and identity.

Navigating Dual Identities:

Individuals within the diaspora often face the challenge of navigating dual identities. Striking a balance between their Eritrean heritage and the cultural nuances of their adopted countries requires a nuanced understanding of identity, cultural pride, and the ability to integrate seamlessly into diverse societies.

Economic Disparities:

Economic disparities within the diaspora community can pose challenges to social cohesion. Addressing income inequalities, providing support to those facing financial difficulties, and fostering economic inclusivity become important components in building a resilient diaspora community.

Mental Health and Well-Being:

The diaspora experience, marked by migration, cultural adaptation, and sometimes displacement, can impact mental health and well-being. Recognizing the importance of mental health support, community-led initiatives, counseling services, and awareness campaigns aim to address the unique challenges faced by diaspora members.

Cultural Preservation Struggles:

Preserving Eritrean culture in a foreign context presents challenges. Diaspora communities actively engage in initiatives to overcome language barriers, adapt traditional practices, and ensure the transmission of cultural heritage to younger generations amid the influences of the diaspora experience.

Community Engagement Barriers:

Engaging the entire diaspora community can be challenging due to diverse backgrounds, experiences, and perspectives. Overcoming barriers to community engagement involves creating inclusive spaces, fostering dialogue, and establishing mechanisms that cater to the needs of all community members.

Adaptive Parenting Styles:

Parents in the diaspora often navigate adaptive parenting styles to address the unique challenges faced by their children. Balancing the preservation of cultural values with the realities of the adopted culture requires a flexible and nuanced approach to parenting within the diaspora context.

Communication Gaps:

Communication gaps, whether generational or stemming from differences in cultural understanding, can strain relationships within the diaspora community. Open and constructive communication becomes pivotal in addressing misunderstandings, fostering unity, and ensuring a harmonious community environment.

Tackling Social Stigmas:

Diaspora members may face social stigmas and stereotypes in their adopted countries. Efforts to challenge and overcome these stigmas involve community-led awareness campaigns, advocacy for inclusivity, and promoting positive narratives that showcase the contributions of the diaspora.

Navigating Legal and Immigration Challenges:

Legal and immigration challenges add an additional layer of complexity to the diaspora experience. Community-led support networks, legal aid initiatives, and advocacy for fair immigration policies become integral components in helping individuals navigate these challenges and build stable lives in their adopted countries.

Fostering Unity Amid Diversity:

The diaspora is diverse, encompassing individuals from various regions, ethnicities, and backgrounds. Fostering unity amid this diversity requires intentional efforts to celebrate differences, promote understanding, and create a sense of shared identity that transcends individual backgrounds.

In the face of these challenges, the Eritrean diaspora exemplifies resilience, drawing strength from its shared history, cultural bonds, and collective aspirations. As families and communities actively navigate these complexities, they contribute to a narrative of strength, adaptability, and the enduring spirit of the Eritrean diaspora.

Cultural Renaissance:

The Eritrean diaspora, dispersed across the globe, is not only a testament to resilience but also a catalyst for a vibrant cultural renaissance. As families and communities navigate the complexities of identity, cultural preservation, and adaptation, the diaspora actively engages in initiatives that breathe new life into Eritrean traditions, arts, and expressions.

Celebrating Heritage:

Cultural associations within the diaspora play a pivotal role in celebrating Eritrean heritage. Through organized events, festivals, and cultural showcases, the diaspora actively preserves and promotes the rich tapestry of Eritrean traditions. These celebrations become platforms for community members to come together, fostering a sense of unity and pride in their shared cultural identity.

Artistic Expressions:

Artists within the diaspora contribute to a burgeoning artistic scene that reflects the diverse experiences and aspirations of Eritrean communities. Whether through music, literature, visual arts, or performing arts, diaspora artists enrich the cultural landscape by infusing traditional elements with contemporary influences, creating a dynamic fusion of creativity.

Preserving Oral Traditions:

In a digital age, the diaspora actively engages in preserving oral traditions. Elders within the community become storytellers, passing down stories, historical narratives, and wisdom to younger generations. Initiatives to document and archive these oral traditions ensure that the cultural heritage of Eritrea continues to thrive and evolve.

Traditional Clothing and Adornments:

The diaspora embraces traditional Eritrean clothing and adornments as symbols of cultural pride. Fashion shows, cultural exhibitions, and community events showcase the vibrant diversity of traditional attire, fostering a sense of connection to Eritrea's rich textile heritage.

Culinary Heritage:

Culinary traditions are actively preserved and celebrated within the diaspora. Eritrean restaurants, culinary events, and cooking workshops become avenues for diaspora members to share and savor the flavors of their homeland. The preparation and enjoyment of traditional dishes serve as communal experiences that connect individuals to their cultural roots.

Language Preservation Initiatives:

Language, a fundamental component of cultural identity, is actively preserved within the diaspora. Language schools, online tutorials, and language immersion programs contribute to the continuity of Tigrinya, Tigre, and other Eritrean languages. This commitment to linguistic heritage strengthens the diaspora's connection to its cultural roots.

Cultural Festivals:

Diaspora communities organize cultural festivals that bring together people from diverse backgrounds to experience the vibrancy of Eritrean culture. These festivals feature music, dance, art, and cultural performances, creating a dynamic and inclusive space where the diaspora can showcase and share its cultural wealth.

Digital Storytelling and Media:

Digital platforms serve as powerful tools for storytelling and media within the diaspora. Online publications, podcasts, and digital media outlets become spaces where Eritrean narratives are shared, providing a platform for diaspora voices to be heard and fostering a sense of community across borders.

Engaging the Youth:

Efforts to engage the youth in cultural preservation are prominent within the diaspora. Youth organizations, cultural exchange programs, and mentorship initiatives ensure that younger generations actively participate in and contribute to the cultural renaissance, infusing fresh perspectives and energy into traditional practices.

Interdisciplinary Collaborations:

Interdisciplinary collaborations become a driving force in the cultural renaissance. Artists, musicians, writers, and scholars collaborate across disciplines, fostering a dynamic cross-pollination of ideas and expressions. These collaborations contribute to the evolution of Eritrean cultural identity within the diaspora.

Revitalizing Folklore and Mythology:

Folklore and mythology are revitalized within the diaspora as storytellers and artists reinterpret and breathe new life into traditional tales. This creative reinterpretation ensures that the essence of Eritrean folklore remains relevant and resonant with contemporary audiences.

Community-Led Educational Initiatives:

Educational initiatives within the diaspora focus on cultural education and awareness. Language schools, cultural exchange programs, and workshops become platforms for community members to learn about their heritage, fostering a deep understanding and appreciation for the cultural richness of Eritrea.

Digital Archives and Museums:

Digital platforms are utilized to create archives and museums that preserve and showcase Eritrean artifacts, historical documents, and cultural artifacts. These digital repositories become accessible resources for the diaspora community, fostering a sense of connection to the past and providing avenues for exploration and learning.

As the Eritrean diaspora actively engages in this cultural renaissance, it becomes a dynamic force for the preservation, adaptation, and evolution of Eritrean cultural identity. Through art, language, culinary traditions, and collaborative initiatives, the diaspora shapes a narrative of cultural continuity that transcends borders and resonates with the shared experiences of Eritreans around the world.

Conclusion:

The impact of the Eritrean diaspora on families and communities is a dynamic tapestry of connections, challenges, and aspirations. From virtual reunions that transcend borders to economic contributions that support livelihoods, the diaspora actively shapes the narrative of Eritrea's future. As families navigate generational dynamics and communities advocate for positive change, the resilience and cultural richness of the diaspora become integral elements in the ongoing story of Eritrea.

Chapter Six

Activism and Advocacy

6.1 Human Rights Advocacy:

The Eritrean diaspora emerges as a powerful force in the global arena, advocating for human rights within their homeland. Activist groups, composed of diaspora members, collaborate with international organizations to shed light on human rights abuses, arbitrary detentions, and the suppression of free expression in Eritrea. Through campaigns, petitions, and awareness initiatives, the diaspora becomes a vocal advocate for the protection and promotion of human rights.

6.2 Political Engagement:

Political organizations within the diaspora actively engage in advocating for political change in Eritrea. Calls for democratic governance, constitutional reforms, and citizen participation resonate within diaspora communities. Through lobbying efforts, outreach campaigns, and collaboration with international policymakers, the diaspora works towards creating a political landscape that reflects the aspirations of the Eritrean people.

6.3 Global Collaboration:

The diaspora engages in global collaborations to address shared challenges and advocate for positive change. From humanitarian crises to public health emergencies, diaspora networks contribute to international efforts. Through partnerships with governments, NGOs, and international institutions, the diaspora amplifies its impact, advocating for policies that address the needs of Eritreans both within the country and in diaspora communities.

6.4 Cultural Diplomacy:

Cultural diplomacy becomes a strategic tool in advocacy efforts. Diaspora communities organize cultural events, exhibitions, and performances that showcase the rich heritage of Eritrea. These initiatives serve not only to celebrate cultural identity but also to foster understanding, dispel stereotypes, and build bridges with the international community.

6.5 Media Initiatives:

Media outlets within the diaspora become platforms for advocacy and information dissemination. Online publications, podcasts, and digital media channels amplify the voices of activists, provide critical analysis of political developments, and offer alternative narratives to counter misinformation. The diaspora leverages the power of media to shape public discourse and raise awareness on issues affecting Eritrea.

6.6 Humanitarian Aid and Relief Efforts:

In response to humanitarian challenges within Eritrea, the diaspora mobilizes to provide aid and relief. Diaspora-led initiatives focus on healthcare, education, and infrastructure development. Collaborating with international humanitarian organizations, the diaspora contributes to alleviating the impact of crises and creating sustainable solutions for communities in need.

6.7 Women and Youth Empowerment:

Empowering women and youth becomes a central focus of diaspora activism. Initiatives promoting gender equality, education for girls, and opportunities for youth empowerment are championed. Through advocacy campaigns, mentorship programs, and collaborative projects, the diaspora works towards creating a more inclusive and equitable society for future generations.

6.8 Environmental Advocacy:

Recognizing the global importance of environmental sustainability, the diaspora engages in advocacy for eco-friendly practices within Eritrea. From tree-planting initiatives to awareness campaigns on climate change, the diaspora contributes to building a greener and more sustainable future for the country.

6.9 Engaging with International Institutions:

The diaspora actively engages with international institutions to draw attention to the challenges faced by Eritreans. Through participation in forums, conferences, and diplomatic channels, diaspora representatives advocate for policies that prioritize the well-being of Eritreans, foster democracy, and address the root causes of displacement.

6.10 Diaspora-Led Development Projects:

Diaspora-led development projects play a crucial role in shaping the future of Eritrea. From healthcare infrastructure to educational initiatives, the diaspora invests in projects that address the immediate needs of communities. By fostering self-reliance and sustainable development, these projects contribute to the long-term prosperity of the homeland.

6.11 Advocacy for Return and Reintegration:

Some within the diaspora advocate for the possibility of return and reintegration into Eritrea. Initiatives focus on creating conditions that would allow diaspora members to return, invest, and contribute to the development of their homeland. These efforts involve dialogue with Eritrean authorities and the international community to address concerns and facilitate a smooth reintegration process.

6.12 Balancing Activism and Diplomacy:

The diaspora grapples with the delicate balance between activism and diplomacy. While advocating for change and raising awareness on human rights abuses, the diaspora also navigates diplomatic channels to foster dialogue and collaboration. This nuanced approach seeks to create a space for constructive engagement while maintaining a commitment to principles of justice and human rights.

In the realm of activism and advocacy, the Eritrean diaspora emerges as a dynamic force, tirelessly working towards positive change, justice, and the well-being of their homeland. Through a multi-faceted approach that encompasses human rights, political engagement, cultural diplomacy, and collaborative initiatives, the diaspora plays a pivotal role in shaping the narrative of Eritrea's future.

In details,

Human Rights Advocacy:

Within the Eritrean diaspora, a passionate commitment to human rights advocacy has emerged as a driving force. Diaspora members, deeply concerned about the situation in their homeland, actively engage in campaigns, awareness initiatives, and collaborations with international organizations to shed light on human rights abuses in Eritrea.

Campaigns for Justice:

Diaspora-led campaigns for justice aim to bring attention to human rights violations within Eritrea. Through social media, grassroots movements, and collaboration with advocacy groups, the diaspora amplifies the voices of those affected, demanding accountability for perpetrators of abuse and seeking justice for victims.

International Partnerships:

Building international partnerships is a key strategy for diaspora human rights advocates. Collaborating with human rights organizations, legal experts, and international institutions, the diaspora works to mobilize global support and resources to address the complex challenges facing Eritreans within the country.

Awareness Initiatives:

Raising awareness about human rights abuses in Eritrea is a central focus of diaspora advocacy. Through informational campaigns, webinars, and public events, the diaspora strives to educate the international community, policymakers, and the general public about the gravity of the human rights situation in Eritrea.

Testimony and Witness Accounts:

Diaspora members actively collect and share testimonies and witness accounts of human rights abuses. These personal narratives serve as powerful tools to humanize the experiences of victims and provide compelling evidence of the need for urgent action to address systemic issues within Eritrea.

Engagement with International Media:

Engaging with international media outlets, the diaspora ensures that the human rights situation in Eritrea receives sustained coverage. Op-eds, interviews, and documentaries featuring diaspora voices contribute to a broader understanding of the challenges faced by Eritreans and garner international attention for the need for change.

Advocacy for Political Prisoners:

A central focus of human rights advocacy within the diaspora is the plight of political prisoners in Eritrea. Diaspora activists tirelessly advocate for the release of individuals detained for expressing dissenting opinions, engaging in political activities, or advocating for democratic reforms.

Mobilizing the International Community:

Diaspora members mobilize the international community through petitions, letters, and direct engagement with policymakers. Advocacy efforts aim to encourage governments, intergovernmental organizations, and institutions to prioritize human rights in their diplomatic relations with Eritrea.

Supporting Refugees and Asylum Seekers:

Human rights advocacy extends to supporting Eritrean refugees and asylum seekers who have fled persecution. The diaspora actively collaborates with refugee support organizations, providing resources, legal assistance, and a platform for displaced individuals to share their experiences and seek refuge.

Legal Initiatives and Accountability:

Diaspora-led legal initiatives seek to hold perpetrators of human rights abuses accountable. This involves exploring legal avenues, working with international human rights lawyers, and supporting efforts to bring cases before international courts or tribunals.

Solidarity with Civil Society:

The diaspora stands in solidarity with Eritrean civil society groups working to promote human rights. Providing financial support, amplifying their voices, and collaborating on joint initiatives, the diaspora actively contributes to the resilience and impact of grassroots movements within Eritrea.

Lobbying for Policy Changes:

Advocacy within the diaspora extends to lobbying for policy changes in the countries where diaspora members reside. Through engagement with elected officials, policymakers, and government bodies, the diaspora seeks to influence foreign policies that address human rights concerns and encourage positive change in Eritrea.

Cultural Expressions for Advocacy:

Cultural expressions, including art, music, and literature, become powerful tools for human rights advocacy. Diaspora artists create works that convey the human experience in Eritrea, bringing attention to the struggles faced by individuals and inspiring empathy and action.

Digital Activism:

Leveraging the power of digital platforms, the diaspora engages in online activism. Social media campaigns, hashtags, and digital storytelling initiatives contribute to a global dialogue on human rights in Eritrea, connecting diaspora members and allies in a collective effort for change.

As the Eritrean diaspora engages in human rights advocacy, it becomes a formidable force for justice, accountability, and the protection of fundamental freedoms. Through a combination of grassroots mobilization, international collaboration, and creative expressions, the diaspora actively contributes to the global movement for human rights and the pursuit of a more just and democratic Eritrea.

Political Engagement:

Political engagement is a cornerstone of the Eritrean diaspora's efforts to shape the future of their homeland. Diaspora members, deeply invested in democratic governance and political reform, actively participate in advocacy, lobbying, and collaborative initiatives to influence positive changes within Eritrea.

Democratic Governance Advocacy:

Diaspora groups advocate for democratic governance in Eritrea, emphasizing the importance of inclusive political processes, transparent institutions, and citizen participation. Through campaigns, discussions, and engagement with international stakeholders, the diaspora promotes a vision of governance that respects human rights, fosters political pluralism, and ensures accountability.

Constitutional Reforms:

The diaspora calls for constitutional reforms in Eritrea, seeking to establish a legal framework that guarantees fundamental rights, separation of powers, and democratic principles. Advocacy efforts focus on encouraging dialogue and collaboration between the government and opposition groups to facilitate a transparent and inclusive constitutional drafting process.

Citizen Participation Initiatives:

Encouraging citizen participation is a central tenet of political engagement within the diaspora. Through awareness campaigns, civic education programs, and community forums, diaspora members empower Eritreans to actively engage in political processes, advocate for their rights, and contribute to the democratic development of their homeland.

Lobbying for International Support:

Diaspora members engage in lobbying efforts to garner international support for political reforms in Eritrea. Through meetings with policymakers, participation in advocacy campaigns, and collaboration with international human rights organizations, the diaspora seeks to build a global coalition advocating for positive political changes.

Supporting Political Opposition:

The diaspora actively supports political opposition groups that align with the principles of democracy and human rights. Through financial contributions, awareness campaigns, and diplomatic efforts, diaspora members work to strengthen opposition movements and create a unified front advocating for political reform.

Collaboration with International Organizations:

Collaboration with international organizations is a key strategy for the diaspora's political engagement. Building alliances with NGOs, think tanks, and institutions dedicated to democracy promotion enhances the diaspora's capacity to influence international policies and frameworks that impact the political landscape in Eritrea.

Promoting Inclusive Dialogue:

Advocating for inclusive dialogue is a crucial aspect of political engagement. The diaspora encourages all stakeholders, including the government, opposition groups, civil society, and citizens, to participate in open and constructive dialogues. The goal is to create a platform for diverse voices to be heard, fostering understanding and collaboration.

Youth Political Empowerment:

Recognizing the vital role of youth in shaping the future, the diaspora focuses on empowering young Eritreans to actively engage in political processes. Youth-led initiatives, mentorship programs, and educational campaigns aim to cultivate a new generation of leaders who are committed to democratic values and civic participation.

Advocacy for Rule of Law:

Diaspora members advocate for the establishment and adherence to the rule of law in Eritrea. Emphasizing the importance of an independent judiciary, accountability mechanisms, and the protection of citizens' rights, the diaspora works to create a legal framework that upholds democratic principles.

Peacebuilding and Reconciliation:

Political engagement within the diaspora includes efforts towards peacebuilding and reconciliation. Advocacy for dialogue between conflicting parties, initiatives to address historical grievances, and support for transitional justice processes contribute to creating a foundation for lasting peace and political stability in Eritrea.

Promoting Women in Politics:

Recognizing the importance of gender equality in political processes, the diaspora advocates for the increased participation of women in politics. Initiatives focus on breaking gender barriers, providing leadership training, and creating an inclusive political environment that values and incorporates the perspectives of women.

Monitoring and Reporting:

Diaspora groups engage in monitoring and reporting on political developments in Eritrea. Through research, fact-finding missions, and collaboration with human rights organizations, the diaspora provides accurate and timely information to the international community, shedding light on political dynamics within the country.

Digital Activism for Political Change:

Leveraging digital platforms, the diaspora engages in online activism to advocate for political change. Social media campaigns, virtual town halls, and digital storytelling initiatives create spaces for diaspora members to express their views, connect with a global audience, and mobilize support for political reform.

As the Eritrean diaspora actively engages in political processes, it becomes a dynamic force for democratic governance, civic participation, and positive political change. Through a combination of advocacy, collaboration, and grassroots initiatives, the diaspora contributes to shaping a political landscape in Eritrea that reflects the aspirations of its people.

Global Collaboration:

Global collaboration is a pivotal aspect of the Eritrean diaspora's efforts to address shared challenges, advocate for positive change, and contribute to international initiatives. Engaging with a diverse range of actors on the global stage, the diaspora actively participates in collaborative endeavors that extend beyond geographic boundaries.

Multilateral Partnerships:

The diaspora actively seeks partnerships with multilateral institutions, such as the United Nations, the African Union, and regional organizations. By engaging with these entities, diaspora members contribute to discussions on human rights, peacebuilding, and development in Eritrea, fostering a multilateral approach to addressing complex issues.

NGO Collaborations:

Collaboration with non-governmental organizations (NGOs) is a cornerstone of the diaspora's global engagement. By working with NGOs focused on human rights, development, and humanitarian aid, the diaspora enhances its capacity to address pressing issues and implement impactful initiatives within Eritrea.

International Development Agencies:

Engagement with international development agencies is a strategic avenue for the diaspora to contribute to sustainable development efforts in Eritrea. By collaborating with agencies such as the World Bank, USAID, and others, the diaspora supports initiatives that aim to alleviate poverty, improve infrastructure, and enhance the overall well-being of communities.

Diaspora Networks and Alliances:

Diaspora networks and alliances play a crucial role in fostering collaboration. By connecting with other diaspora communities, particularly those with shared experiences, the Eritrean diaspora strengthens its global influence. Collaborative initiatives may include joint advocacy campaigns, cultural exchanges, and support for common causes.

Global Advocacy Campaigns:

Participation in global advocacy campaigns amplifies the diaspora's voice on critical issues. Whether addressing human rights abuses, advocating for democratic reforms, or promoting sustainable development, the diaspora collaborates with international advocacy groups to create global movements that garner attention and support.

International Conferences and Forums:

Active participation in international conferences and forums provides the diaspora with opportunities to share insights, discuss challenges, and build alliances. Diaspora representatives contribute to discussions on Eritrea's political landscape, human rights, and development, fostering a nuanced understanding of the complexities facing the country.

Collaborative Research and Data Sharing:

Collaborative research initiatives enable the diaspora to contribute valuable insights and data to the global knowledge base. By partnering with research institutions, think tanks, and academic organizations, the diaspora actively engages in studies that inform international policies and strategies related to Eritrea.

Peacebuilding Initiatives:

Global collaboration extends to peacebuilding initiatives, where the diaspora actively engages in efforts to promote reconciliation and conflict resolution. Collaborative projects may involve partnerships with international peacebuilding organizations, fostering dialogue between conflicting parties, and contributing to the establishment of sustainable peace in Eritrea.

Humanitarian Alliances:

In times of humanitarian crises, the diaspora collaborates with international humanitarian alliances to provide timely and effective assistance. Whether responding to natural disasters or addressing the needs of displaced populations, collaborative efforts ensure a coordinated and impactful response.

Cultural Diplomacy Programs:

Cultural diplomacy becomes a powerful tool for global collaboration. Through cultural exchange programs, art exhibitions, and performances, the diaspora engages with international audiences to foster understanding, dispel stereotypes, and promote a positive image of Eritrean culture and heritage.

Collaboration with International Media:

Engaging with international media outlets facilitates a broader dissemination of information and perspectives. The diaspora collaborates with journalists, filmmakers, and media organizations to share stories, raise awareness, and shape narratives that contribute to a nuanced understanding of Eritrea on the global stage.

Participation in Global Initiatives:

The diaspora actively participates in global initiatives aligned with its values and objectives. Whether contributing to sustainable development goals, participating in global campaigns for justice, or supporting international efforts for peace, the diaspora plays a role in shaping a positive and inclusive global agenda.

Digital Collaboration Platforms:

Leveraging digital collaboration platforms, the diaspora engages in virtual initiatives that connect members across borders. Online forums, webinars, and collaborative digital projects create spaces for real-time collaboration, enabling the diaspora to work collectively on shared goals.

Through global collaboration, the Eritrean diaspora becomes a dynamic force that transcends geographic boundaries, contributing to a collective effort to address challenges, advocate for positive change, and shape a brighter future for Eritrea on the international stage.

Cultural Diplomacy:

Cultural diplomacy emerges as a strategic and impactful tool within the Eritrean diaspora's efforts to build bridges, foster understanding, and promote a positive image of Eritrea on the global stage. Through various cultural initiatives, diaspora members actively engage in diplomatic endeavors that transcend political boundaries and contribute to a more interconnected world.

Cultural Showcases and Festivals:

The diaspora organizes cultural showcases and festivals that highlight the richness and diversity of Eritrean traditions. These events, featuring music, dance, art, and culinary delights, serve as vibrant platforms for cultural exchange. By inviting diverse audiences to experience Eritrean culture, the diaspora fosters understanding and appreciation.

Art Exhibitions and Galleries:

Visual arts become a medium for cultural diplomacy, with diaspora artists contributing to international art scenes. Art exhibitions and galleries showcase Eritrean talent, providing a unique lens through which audiences can explore the narratives, expressions, and perspectives embedded in Eritrean art.

Film and Documentary Screenings:

Film and documentary screenings present a powerful avenue for cultural diplomacy. Diaspora filmmakers produce works that delve into the complexities of Eritrean identity, history, and contemporary issues. Screenings at international film festivals and events facilitate cross-cultural dialogue and challenge stereotypes.

Literary Events and Book Launches:

Diaspora authors and writers contribute to the global literary landscape, sharing Eritrean stories through novels, poetry, and essays. Literary events and book launches provide opportunities for diaspora writers to engage with international audiences, fostering a deeper understanding of Eritrean narratives.

Language and Educational Programs:

Promoting Eritrean languages through language schools and educational programs becomes a form of cultural diplomacy. The diaspora actively engages with academic institutions, language institutes, and community-based initiatives to preserve and promote Tigrinya, Tigre, and other Eritrean languages.

Cultural Diplomacy through Cuisine:

Eritrean cuisine serves as a cultural ambassador, with diaspora chefs and culinary enthusiasts sharing the flavors of Eritrea worldwide. Restaurants, culinary events, and cooking workshops become spaces where individuals can savor traditional Eritrean dishes, fostering cultural exchange through the universal language of food.

Collaborative Cultural Projects:

Collaborative cultural projects bring together artists, musicians, writers, and performers from the diaspora and other communities. These cross-cultural collaborations produce works that transcend borders, celebrating the interconnectedness of diverse cultural expressions and promoting unity through shared artistic endeavors.

Youth Exchange Programs:

Youth exchange programs create opportunities for young Eritreans in the diaspora to engage with their peers from different cultural backgrounds. These programs foster cross-cultural friendships, promote intercultural dialogue, and contribute to a generation that values diversity and global interconnectedness.

Digital Platforms for Cultural Exchange:

Leveraging digital platforms, the diaspora engages in virtual cultural exchange initiatives. Online forums, virtual exhibitions, and digital storytelling projects enable real-time interaction, allowing individuals from around the world to connect with Eritrean culture and heritage.

Cultural Diplomacy in Education:

Engaging with educational institutions, the diaspora promotes cultural diplomacy through guest lectures, workshops, and educational partnerships. These initiatives aim to integrate

Eritrean perspectives into curricula, fostering a more inclusive and nuanced understanding of the country's history and culture.

Participation in International Arts and Culture Networks:

Diaspora artists and cultural ambassadors actively participate in international arts and culture networks. By collaborating with global organizations, participating in cultural exchange programs, and contributing to cross-cultural dialogues, the diaspora strengthens its influence in the global cultural arena.

Diaspora-Led Cultural Diplomacy Organizations:

The establishment of diaspora-led cultural diplomacy organizations becomes a strategic initiative. These organizations serve as hubs for coordinating cultural initiatives, facilitating collaborations, and promoting Eritrean culture as a positive and enriching force in the global cultural landscape.

Promotion of Traditional Clothing and Adornments:

Traditional Eritrean clothing and adornments become symbols of cultural pride and diplomacy. Fashion shows, cultural exhibitions, and collaborations with international designers showcase the beauty and significance of traditional attire, fostering cross-cultural appreciation.

Through cultural diplomacy, the Eritrean diaspora actively contributes to shaping a positive global perception of Eritrea. By leveraging the universal language of culture, diaspora members build bridges, create spaces for dialogue, and promote a more interconnected world that values and celebrates the diversity of cultural expressions.

Media Initiatives:

Media initiatives within the Eritrean diaspora play a crucial role in shaping narratives, raising awareness, and fostering dialogue on a global scale. From online platforms to traditional media outlets, the diaspora leverages various forms of media to amplify its voice, share stories, and engage with international audiences.

Online Publications and Blogs:

Diaspora members contribute to online publications and blogs that serve as platforms for in-depth analyses, personal narratives, and commentary on Eritrean issues. These digital spaces enable the diaspora to share diverse perspectives, challenge stereotypes, and provide nuanced insights into the complexities of Eritrea.

Podcasts and Digital Audio Platforms:

Podcasts become a dynamic medium for diaspora voices to be heard. Podcasters within the diaspora produce content that covers a range of topics, including history, culture, human rights, and current affairs. These digital audio platforms create accessible spaces for storytelling, interviews, and discussions.

YouTube Channels and Video Content:

YouTube channels hosted by diaspora members feature video content that spans cultural showcases, documentaries, interviews, and vlogs. Video content becomes a powerful tool for visual storytelling, allowing the diaspora to convey the vibrancy of Eritrean culture, highlight important issues, and reach diverse audiences.

Documentary Productions:

Diaspora filmmakers produce documentaries that delve into the historical, social, and political aspects of Eritrea. These documentary productions contribute to a deeper understanding of the country's complexities, shedding light on human rights issues, historical narratives, and the experiences of Eritreans both within the country and in the diaspora.

Print Magazines and Periodicals:

Print magazines and periodicals provide a tangible platform for diaspora members to share narratives, conduct interviews, and explore various aspects of Eritrean culture. These publications serve as informative resources that contribute to a more comprehensive understanding of the Eritrean diaspora experience.

Collaboration with International Media Outlets:

Engaging with international media outlets, the diaspora actively collaborates to share Eritrean perspectives on global platforms. Interviews, op-eds, and feature articles contribute to a more nuanced representation of Eritrea and its diaspora in mainstream media, challenging stereotypes and promoting accurate narratives.

Digital Storytelling Platforms:

Digital storytelling platforms become channels through which diaspora members share personal narratives, experiences, and reflections. Through written, visual, and multimedia storytelling, individuals within the diaspora create a mosaic of voices that collectively contribute to a richer understanding of the Eritrean diaspora's diverse stories.

Social Media Campaigns:

Leveraging social media platforms, the diaspora engages in impactful campaigns that raise awareness on human rights issues, political developments, and cultural celebrations. Hashtags, viral campaigns, and coordinated efforts amplify diaspora voices, reaching a global audience and fostering dialogue on pressing issues.

Diaspora Radio Stations:

Diaspora radio stations provide a platform for Eritrean voices to be heard through music, talk shows, and news broadcasts. These stations become community hubs, fostering a sense of connection among diaspora members while also serving as informative outlets for the broader public.

Collaborative Media Projects:

Collaborative media projects bring together diaspora journalists, content creators, and storytellers to produce impactful narratives. These projects may include multimedia initiatives, investigative journalism, and cross-cultural collaborations that contribute to a more comprehensive and nuanced portrayal of Eritrean stories.

Digital Magazines and Online Journals:

Digital magazines and online journals become vehicles for in-depth exploration of Eritrean culture, history, and current affairs. Diaspora-led initiatives contribute to these publications, offering diverse perspectives and fostering a space for critical dialogue on the challenges and opportunities facing Eritrea.

Media Literacy and Educational Programs:

Recognizing the importance of media literacy, the diaspora engages in educational programs that promote critical thinking and responsible media consumption. Workshops, webinars, and educational initiatives aim to empower individuals to navigate media landscapes and discern reliable sources of information.

Community Media Centers:

Establishing community media centers becomes a strategic initiative within the diaspora. These centers provide resources, training, and equipment for community members to produce and share their own media content, further diversifying the range of voices within the diaspora narrative.

Through diverse media initiatives, the Eritrean diaspora actively shapes the narrative surrounding Eritrea, fostering understanding, challenging stereotypes, and contributing to a global conversation on the country's history, culture, and the aspirations of its people.

Humanitarian Aid and Relief Efforts:

Recognizing the humanitarian challenges faced by Eritreans both within the country and among displaced communities, the Eritrean diaspora actively engages in humanitarian aid and relief efforts. Through collaborative initiatives and partnerships, diaspora members work towards alleviating the impact of crises and building sustainable solutions for those in need.

Emergency Relief Campaigns:

In response to humanitarian crises, the diaspora organizes emergency relief campaigns to provide immediate assistance to affected communities. These campaigns may include fundraising drives, collection of essential supplies, and coordination with humanitarian organizations to deliver aid to those in distress.

Medical Outreach Programs:

Diaspora healthcare professionals and volunteers organize medical outreach programs to address the healthcare needs of vulnerable populations in Eritrea. These programs may involve medical missions, the provision of medical supplies, and partnerships with local healthcare facilities to enhance access to essential services.

Education and Literacy Initiatives:

Recognizing the importance of education, the diaspora supports initiatives that promote literacy and access to education for Eritrean children and youth. This may include the establishment of schools, distribution of educational materials, and scholarships for students facing financial barriers.

Infrastructure Development Projects:

Diaspora-led infrastructure development projects aim to address the basic needs of communities in Eritrea. This may involve the construction of schools, healthcare facilities, water wells, and other essential infrastructure to improve living conditions and enhance resilience to future challenges.

Refugee Support Programs:

In collaboration with international refugee organizations, the diaspora actively supports Eritrean refugees and asylum seekers. This may include the provision of shelter, legal assistance, psychosocial support, and initiatives that empower refugees to rebuild their lives in host countries.

Clean Water and Sanitation Initiatives:

Access to clean water and sanitation is a fundamental focus of humanitarian efforts. The diaspora engages in projects that aim to improve water infrastructure, provide sanitation facilities, and promote hygiene education to prevent waterborne diseases and enhance the overall well-being of communities.

Nutrition and Food Security Programs:

Addressing food insecurity is a priority for the diaspora, especially in the face of droughts and other challenges. Nutrition programs, agricultural support, and initiatives promoting sustainable farming practices contribute to enhancing food security and resilience among vulnerable populations.

Community Empowerment and Livelihood Projects:

Diaspora-led initiatives prioritize community empowerment and sustainable livelihoods.

Projects may include vocational training, microfinance programs, and support for small businesses, empowering communities to build economic resilience and reduce dependency on external aid.

Women and Youth Empowerment Initiatives:

Recognizing the unique challenges faced by women and youth, the diaspora supports initiatives that empower these demographics. This may involve mentorship programs, skill development workshops, and projects that create opportunities for women and youth to actively participate in community development.

Psychosocial Support and Mental Health Services:

Humanitarian efforts extend to addressing the psychosocial well-being of individuals affected by crises. The diaspora collaborates with mental health professionals to provide counseling services, support groups, and awareness campaigns to reduce the stigma associated with mental health issues.

Climate Resilience and Environmental Conservation:

Acknowledging the impact of climate change, the diaspora engages in projects focused on climate resilience and environmental conservation. Tree-planting initiatives, sustainable agriculture practices, and educational programs contribute to building environmental resilience and mitigating the effects of climate-related challenges.

Collaboration with International NGOs:

The diaspora actively collaborates with international non-governmental organizations (NGOs) to leverage resources, expertise, and networks. These collaborations enhance the impact of humanitarian initiatives and ensure a coordinated response to complex challenges facing Eritrean communities.

Advocacy for Humanitarian Assistance:

Beyond direct involvement in aid delivery, the diaspora engages in advocacy efforts to raise awareness about humanitarian challenges in Eritrea. By collaborating with international organizations, governments, and the media, diaspora members work to mobilize support for sustained humanitarian assistance and long-term solutions.

Participation in Global Health Initiatives:

In the face of health challenges, the diaspora actively participates in global health initiatives. This may involve collaborations with international health organizations, contributions to healthcare research, and advocacy for policies that prioritize the health and well-being of Eritrean communities.

Through these humanitarian aid and relief efforts, the Eritrean diaspora demonstrates a commitment to addressing immediate needs, building resilience, and contributing to sustainable development in Eritrea and among displaced Eritrean communities worldwide.

Humanitarian Aid and Relief Efforts:

The Eritrean diaspora, driven by a deep commitment to addressing the pressing humanitarian needs of their fellow Eritreans, has been actively engaged in a variety of humanitarian aid and relief efforts. These initiatives are designed to provide immediate assistance to those facing crises, as well as to contribute to the long-term development and resilience of communities in Eritrea and beyond.

1. Emergency Relief Campaigns:

Diaspora-led emergency relief campaigns mobilize resources, including financial aid and essential supplies, to respond swiftly to crises such as natural disasters, conflict, or other emergencies.

Coordination with international humanitarian organizations ensures efficient and targeted distribution of aid to affected communities.

2. Medical Outreach Programs:

Healthcare professionals within the diaspora organize medical outreach programs to address the healthcare needs of vulnerable populations.

Medical missions, provision of medical supplies, and partnerships with local healthcare facilities enhance access to essential health services.

3. Education and Literacy Initiatives:

The diaspora supports initiatives promoting literacy and education in Eritrea, including the establishment of schools, distribution of educational materials, and scholarship programs.

Education is viewed as a key component for long-term community development and empowerment.

4. Infrastructure Development Projects:

Diaspora-led projects focus on improving basic infrastructure, such as the construction of schools, healthcare facilities, and water wells.

Sustainable infrastructure development aims to enhance living conditions and build resilience in communities.

5. Refugee Support Programs:

Collaboration with international refugee organizations enables the diaspora to support Eritrean refugees and asylum seekers.

Activities include providing shelter, legal assistance, and initiatives empowering refugees to rebuild their lives in host countries.

6. Clean Water and Sanitation Initiatives:

Projects targeting water infrastructure improvement, sanitation facilities, and hygiene education aim to prevent waterborne diseases and enhance overall well-being.

Access to clean water and sanitation is considered fundamental for community health.

7. Nutrition and Food Security Programs:

The diaspora addresses food insecurity through nutrition programs, agricultural support, and sustainable farming initiatives.

These programs contribute to enhancing food security and building resilience against challenges like droughts.

8. Community Empowerment and Livelihood Projects:

Initiatives promoting community empowerment and sustainable livelihoods include vocational training, microfinance programs, and support for small businesses.

Economic empowerment is viewed as essential for reducing dependency on external aid.

9. Women and Youth Empowerment Initiatives:

Specialized programs focus on empowering women and youth through mentorship, skill development, and opportunities for active participation in community development.

Recognizing the unique challenges faced by these demographics, empowerment initiatives aim to create inclusive and resilient communities.

10. Psychosocial Support and Mental Health Services:

Collaborations with mental health professionals result in counseling services, support groups, and awareness campaigns to address the psychosocial well-being of affected individuals.

Reducing the stigma associated with mental health issues is a key aspect of these initiatives.

11. Climate Resilience and Environmental Conservation:

Projects centered around climate resilience and environmental conservation include tree-planting initiatives and sustainable agriculture practices.

Acknowledging the impact of climate change, these initiatives aim to build environmental resilience.

12. Collaboration with International NGOs:

Active collaboration with international non-governmental organizations (NGOs) enhances the impact and reach of humanitarian initiatives.

Networking and partnership building contribute to a coordinated and effective response to complex challenges.

13. Advocacy for Humanitarian Assistance:

Beyond direct involvement, the diaspora engages in advocacy efforts to raise awareness about humanitarian challenges in Eritrea.

Collaboration with international organizations, governments, and media helps mobilize support for sustained humanitarian assistance.

14. Participation in Global Health Initiatives:

The diaspora actively participates in global health initiatives, collaborating with international health organizations and advocating for policies prioritizing health and well-being.

Contributions to healthcare research and awareness campaigns are part of these efforts.

Through these multifaceted humanitarian aid and relief efforts, the Eritrean diaspora contributes significantly to alleviating immediate challenges and fostering sustainable development, resilience, and empowerment within Eritrea and among displaced Eritrean communities worldwide.

Women and Youth Empowerment:

Recognizing the unique challenges faced by women and youth, the Eritrean diaspora actively engages in initiatives aimed at empowerment, education, and creating opportunities for these demographics. Through targeted programs and collaborative efforts, the diaspora strives to uplift women and youth, fostering their leadership, education, and socio-economic well-being.

1. Educational Empowerment:

Scholarship programs and educational initiatives specifically target young girls and women, ensuring access to quality education.

Workshops and mentorship programs empower youth by providing them with the skills and knowledge necessary for personal and professional development.

2. Vocational Training and Skill Development:

The diaspora supports vocational training programs that equip both women and youth with practical skills, enhancing their employability and entrepreneurial capabilities.

Skill development initiatives address the unique needs and aspirations of these demographics, opening avenues for economic independence.

3. Entrepreneurship and Small Business Support:

Initiatives focus on supporting women and youth in entrepreneurship, offering mentorship, access to funding, and resources to start and grow small businesses.

Entrepreneurial ventures contribute not only to economic empowerment but also to community development.

4. Leadership Development Programs:

Leadership development programs target both women and youth, providing training in leadership skills, communication, and community engagement.

These programs aim to foster a new generation of leaders who actively contribute to the social and political development of Eritrea.

5. Health and Wellness Initiatives:

Women's and youth health programs prioritize access to healthcare services, reproductive health education, and mental health support.

Promoting holistic well-being is a key focus, acknowledging the intersectionality of health with other aspects of empowerment.

6. Advocacy for Women's and Youth Rights:

Diaspora members actively engage in advocacy for the rights of women and youth, participating in campaigns and initiatives that address issues such as gender equality, education access, and youth participation in decision-making processes.

Advocacy efforts aim to influence policies and societal norms for the benefit of these demographics.

7. Cultural and Artistic Empowerment:

Cultural and artistic initiatives provide platforms for women and youth to express themselves creatively, fostering a sense of identity and empowerment.

Participation in cultural events, art exhibitions, and performances contributes to the preservation of cultural heritage and the celebration of diverse talents.

8. Mentorship Programs:

The diaspora establishes mentorship programs that connect experienced professionals with young women and men, providing guidance and support in various fields.

Mentorship relationships play a crucial role in nurturing talent and fostering a sense of community and belonging.

9. Sports and Recreation Programs:

Engagement in sports and recreation programs promotes physical well-being, teamwork, and discipline among youth.

Sporting events and activities provide avenues for personal growth, skill development, and the cultivation of a strong community spirit.

10. Civic Engagement and Participation:

Encouraging civic engagement, the diaspora supports initiatives that promote youth participation in community decision-making and political processes.

Empowering youth to actively contribute to shaping the future of Eritrea is a central goal of these initiatives.

11. Networking and Community Building:

Networking events and community-building initiatives create spaces for women and youth to connect, share experiences, and support each other.

Building strong community ties enhances resilience and provides a supportive environment for personal and collective growth.

12. Digital Literacy Programs:

Recognizing the importance of digital literacy, the diaspora supports programs that equip women and youth with digital skills.

Access to technology and digital literacy enhances educational and economic opportunities, contributing to overall empowerment.

13. Human Rights and Gender Equality Advocacy:

The diaspora actively engages in advocacy for human rights and gender equality, addressing issues such as gender-based violence, discrimination, and unequal opportunities.

Advocacy efforts contribute to shaping a more equitable and inclusive society.

14. Cultural Preservation and Identity Building:

Cultural preservation initiatives focus on transmitting cultural values, traditions, and languages to the younger generation.

Building a strong sense of identity contributes to the empowerment of youth and reinforces the importance of cultural heritage.

Through these comprehensive initiatives, the Eritrean diaspora endeavors to create an environment where women and youth can thrive, lead, and contribute to the social, economic, and cultural vibrancy of Eritrea and its diaspora communities worldwide.

Environmental Advocacy:

Recognizing the critical importance of environmental sustainability, the Eritrean diaspora actively engages in environmental advocacy initiatives. These efforts focus on raising awareness, promoting conservation, and implementing sustainable practices to address environmental challenges within Eritrea and contribute to global environmental stewardship.

1. Tree-Planting Campaigns:

Diaspora-led tree-planting campaigns contribute to reforestation efforts and combat deforestation, addressing challenges related to soil erosion, biodiversity loss, and climate change.

Community participation and awareness-building activities accompany these campaigns to foster a culture of environmental responsibility.

2. Sustainable Agriculture Initiatives:

Initiatives promoting sustainable agricultural practices aim to improve food security while minimizing the environmental impact of farming activities.

Training programs and support for farmers encourage the adoption of practices that enhance soil health, conserve water, and reduce reliance on chemical inputs.

3. Climate Resilience Programs:

Climate resilience programs address the impact of climate change on vulnerable communities. These initiatives involve the development of strategies to adapt to changing climatic conditions, ensuring the well-being of both people and ecosystems.

4. Plastic Waste Reduction Campaigns:

Advocacy campaigns target the reduction of plastic waste by promoting awareness, encouraging recycling practices, and advocating for policies that minimize single-use plastics.

Community clean-up initiatives contribute to both waste reduction and environmental education.

5. Conservation of Natural Habitats:

Diaspora-led efforts focus on the conservation of natural habitats, including parks, wildlife reserves, and coastal ecosystems.

Support for conservation initiatives helps protect biodiversity, maintain ecological balance, and preserve natural beauty.

6. Water Conservation Programs:

Water conservation programs promote responsible water usage and management, especially in regions facing water scarcity.

Community education, the implementation of water-efficient technologies, and sustainable water resource management are central components of these programs.

7. Renewable Energy Advocacy:

Advocacy for renewable energy sources, such as solar and wind power, aims to reduce reliance on fossil fuels and mitigate the impact of climate change.

Awareness campaigns and support for renewable energy projects contribute to the transition to more sustainable energy practices.

8. Environmental Education and Awareness:

Educational initiatives raise awareness about environmental issues, fostering a sense of responsibility and encouraging sustainable practices.

Workshops, seminars, and awareness campaigns target both communities and individuals, emphasizing the interconnectedness of human well-being with a healthy environment.

9. Erosion Control and Land Restoration:

Diaspora-led projects focus on erosion control and land restoration, employing techniques such as afforestation, terracing, and soil conservation.

These efforts contribute to maintaining fertile land, preventing desertification, and ensuring the long-term productivity of agricultural areas.

10. Marine Conservation Efforts:

Advocacy for marine conservation addresses the protection of coastal ecosystems and marine life.

Collaborative projects may include beach clean-ups, awareness campaigns against overfishing, and support for sustainable fishing practices.

11. Wildlife Protection Initiatives:

Efforts to protect wildlife involve anti-poaching campaigns, habitat preservation, and initiatives to mitigate human-wildlife conflict.

Collaboration with local communities and authorities ensures the sustainable coexistence of human populations and wildlife.

12. Sustainable Urban Planning Advocacy:

Advocacy for sustainable urban planning promotes environmentally friendly infrastructure, green spaces, and energy-efficient practices in urban areas.

Collaborating with urban development authorities and advocating for eco-friendly policies contribute to building resilient and sustainable cities.

13. Community-Based Conservation Projects:

Community-based conservation projects empower local communities to actively participate in the protection and sustainable use of natural resources.

By involving communities in decision-making processes, these projects promote a sense of ownership and responsibility for environmental stewardship.

14. Advocacy for Environmental Policies:

Engaging with policymakers and governmental bodies, the diaspora advocates for the development and implementation of environmentally friendly policies.

Collaboration with environmental organizations and participation in policy discussions contribute to shaping a legislative framework that prioritizes sustainability.

Through these multifaceted environmental advocacy initiatives, the Eritrean diaspora contributes to building a sustainable and resilient future for Eritrea, aligning with global efforts to address the interconnected challenges of climate change and environmental degradation.

Engaging with International Institutions:

Recognizing the significance of global collaboration in addressing the challenges faced by Eritrea, the Eritrean diaspora actively engages with international institutions. These efforts involve diplomatic initiatives, partnerships, and advocacy to garner support, raise awareness, and contribute to shaping policies that positively impact Eritrea and its diaspora communities.

1. Diplomatic Outreach:

Diaspora representatives engage in diplomatic efforts to establish and strengthen relationships with foreign governments, international organizations, and diplomatic missions.

Diplomatic engagements aim to advocate for Eritrean interests, raise awareness about the challenges faced by the country, and foster international collaboration.

2. Human Rights Advocacy:

The diaspora actively participates in human rights advocacy at international forums, drawing attention to issues such as political repression, freedom of expression, and the rights of refugees.

Collaboration with human rights organizations and participation in events like the United Nations Human Rights Council sessions contribute to global conversations on human rights.

3. Economic Partnerships and Investment:

Diaspora members work to establish economic partnerships and attract investments that benefit both Eritrea and its diaspora communities.

Building economic bridges with international institutions, businesses, and investors contributes to economic development and sustainability.

4. Educational and Cultural Exchanges:

Facilitating educational and cultural exchanges, the diaspora collaborates with international academic institutions and cultural organizations.

Exchange programs enhance cultural understanding, create opportunities for Eritrean students, and contribute to a more interconnected global community.

5. Collaboration with International NGOs:

Active collaboration with international non-governmental organizations (NGOs) enhances the impact of diaspora-led initiatives, particularly in humanitarian aid, development projects, and advocacy.

Partnerships with NGOs ensure a coordinated and effective response to challenges faced by Eritrea and its diaspora.

6. Participation in Global Health Initiatives:

Engaging in global health initiatives, the diaspora collaborates with international health organizations to address health challenges and promote well-being.

Contributions to health research, awareness campaigns, and partnerships with health institutions enhance the diaspora's impact in the global health landscape.

7. Environmental Partnerships:

Engaging with international institutions focused on environmental sustainability, the diaspora contributes to global efforts in addressing climate change and environmental degradation.

Partnerships may involve collaborative projects, participation in global environmental conferences, and advocacy for sustainable practices.

8. Advocacy for Policy Change:

Diaspora representatives actively advocate for policy changes at the international level to address issues such as governance, human rights, and economic development in Eritrea.

Participation in policy discussions, engagement with think tanks, and collaboration with policymakers contribute to shaping a positive policy environment.

9. Collaboration with UN Agencies:

Collaboration with United Nations (UN) agencies involves participating in programs, initiatives, and discussions relevant to the challenges faced by Eritrea.

Engaging with UN agencies ensures that the diaspora's perspectives are considered in global efforts to address humanitarian, developmental, and human rights issues.

10. Representation at International Forums:

Diaspora representatives actively participate in international forums, conferences, and summits to voice Eritrean perspectives, share experiences, and contribute to global discussions.

These forums provide platforms to build networks, raise awareness, and advocate for policies that align with the interests of Eritrea and its diaspora.

11. Diaspora-Led Diplomatic Missions:

Organizing diaspora-led diplomatic missions allows for direct engagement with international stakeholders, fostering dialogue, and building relationships.

These missions may involve meetings with government officials, policymakers, and representatives of international organizations to discuss issues pertinent to Eritrea.

12. Collaboration with International Financial Institutions:

Engaging with international financial institutions facilitates access to financial resources, investments, and developmental assistance.

Collaboration with institutions such as the World Bank and International Monetary Fund contributes to economic stability and development.

13. Media Engagement on International Platforms:

Diaspora members actively engage with international media platforms to share perspectives, raise awareness, and shape global narratives about Eritrea.

Media engagement contributes to building a more nuanced and accurate understanding of the challenges and opportunities in Eritrea.

14. Diaspora Contributions to Global Initiatives:

Encouraging diaspora contributions to global initiatives ensures that Eritreans actively participate in international efforts related to sustainable development, peacebuilding, and human rights.

The diaspora becomes a valuable resource in shaping a positive global image of Eritrea and contributing to the achievement of international goals.

Through these diverse avenues of engagement with international institutions, the Eritrean diaspora plays a crucial role in advocating for positive change, fostering collaboration, and contributing to the global discourse on issues affecting Eritrea and its diaspora communities.

Diaspora-Led Development Projects:

Harnessing the skills, resources, and passion of the Eritrean diaspora, various development projects are initiated to address key challenges faced by Eritrea. These projects aim to foster sustainable development, enhance livelihoods, and contribute to the overall well-being of communities within Eritrea and the diaspora. The diaspora-led development projects encompass a wide range of sectors, reflecting a holistic approach to addressing the multifaceted needs of the country.

1. Infrastructure Development:

Diaspora-led initiatives focus on building and improving critical infrastructure such as roads, schools, healthcare facilities, and water supply systems.

Infrastructure projects contribute to enhancing the quality of life, promoting economic development, and ensuring access to essential services.

2. Educational Initiatives:

Collaborative efforts with educational institutions aim to improve access to quality education, including the establishment of schools, provision of educational materials, and scholarship programs.

Investing in education is seen as a key strategy for empowering future generations and fostering sustainable development.

3. Healthcare Access Programs:

Healthcare initiatives involve improving access to medical services, supporting healthcare facilities, and organizing medical missions to address the healthcare needs of vulnerable populations.

These programs contribute to enhancing public health, reducing morbidity, and improving overall well-being.

4. Agricultural Development Projects:

Diaspora-led projects focus on promoting sustainable agricultural practices, providing training to farmers, and supporting initiatives that enhance food security.

Agricultural development contributes to economic stability, rural livelihoods, and resilience against food-related challenges.

5. Economic Empowerment Programs:

Economic empowerment projects include support for small businesses, vocational training programs, and initiatives that create employment opportunities.

By fostering economic resilience, these programs contribute to reducing poverty and improving the livelihoods of individuals and communities.

6. Clean Energy Initiatives:

The diaspora invests in clean energy projects, promoting the use of renewable energy sources such as solar and wind power.

Clean energy initiatives contribute to environmental sustainability while addressing energy needs and promoting economic development.

7. Water and Sanitation Projects:

Projects targeting water and sanitation infrastructure address challenges related to clean water access and hygiene.

These initiatives contribute to improving public health, preventing waterborne diseases, and ensuring sustainable water management.

8. Technology and Innovation Hubs:

Establishing technology and innovation hubs fosters the development of technological skills, entrepreneurship, and innovation within Eritrea.

These hubs become focal points for fostering creativity, supporting startups, and driving technological advancements.

9. Cultural Preservation and Heritage Projects:

Cultural preservation projects aim to safeguard Eritrean heritage by documenting, restoring, and promoting cultural traditions, languages, and historical sites.

Preserving cultural identity is considered essential for the well-being of communities and the promotion of tourism.

10. Women and Youth Empowerment Centers:

Centers dedicated to women and youth empowerment offer a range of services, including education, vocational training, and support for entrepreneurship.

Empowering women and youth is viewed as a catalyst for social and economic development.

11. Microfinance and Financial Inclusion Programs:

Microfinance initiatives provide financial services to individuals who may not have access to traditional banking systems, supporting entrepreneurship and economic development.

Financial inclusion programs contribute to building a more resilient and economically vibrant society.

12. Community-Based Conservation Projects:

Conservation projects involve local communities in efforts to preserve natural habitats, protect biodiversity, and address environmental challenges.

These community-based initiatives promote environmental stewardship and sustainable resource management.

13. Diaspora Health and Wellness Clinics:

Establishing health and wellness clinics allows the diaspora to directly contribute to healthcare delivery, including preventive care, health education, and community outreach.

These clinics enhance access to healthcare services and promote overall well-being.

14. Entrepreneurship and Innovation Incubators:

Entrepreneurship and innovation incubators provide support for startups, fostering a culture of innovation and creativity.

These initiatives contribute to economic diversification and job creation.

Through the implementation of these diaspora-led development projects, the Eritrean diaspora actively participates in shaping a more sustainable, resilient, and prosperous future for

Eritrea and its communities, both within the country and around the world.

Advocacy for Return and Reintegration:

Recognizing the importance of fostering connections between the Eritrean diaspora and their homeland, advocacy for return and reintegration initiatives aims to create pathways for diaspora members to contribute to the development of Eritrea while reintegrating into their communities. These advocacy efforts focus on addressing challenges and creating an enabling environment for a successful return and meaningful reintegration.

1. Diaspora Engagement Platforms:

Advocacy involves the creation of platforms that facilitate communication and collaboration between the diaspora and Eritrea.

Online forums, community events, and networking platforms provide spaces for dialogue, idea-sharing, and fostering a sense of community.

2. Recognition of Diaspora Contributions:

Advocacy emphasizes the recognition of the valuable contributions made by the diaspora, both in their host countries and through remittances.

Acknowledging these contributions fosters a sense of appreciation and encourages diaspora members to actively engage in the development of Eritrea.

3. Policy Advocacy for Reintegration:

Diaspora-led advocacy efforts target the development and implementation of policies that support the reintegration of returnees.

Collaborating with government agencies, advocacy aims to create an environment that welcomes returnees and provides necessary support systems.

4. Skills Transfer and Capacity Building:

Advocacy focuses on initiatives that promote the transfer of skills and knowledge from the diaspora to local communities.

Skill development programs and capacity-building initiatives create opportunities for the diaspora to contribute their expertise to various sectors in Eritrea.

5. Investment Promotion:

Advocacy encourages policies and initiatives that attract diaspora investments in key sectors, including infrastructure, healthcare, and education.

Investment promotion contributes to economic development and job creation, fostering sustainable growth.

6. Recognition of Dual Identity:

Advocacy efforts promote the recognition and acceptance of dual identities among diaspora members who return to Eritrea.

Acknowledging and celebrating cultural diversity contributes to a more inclusive and welcoming society.

7. Legal and Regulatory Support:

Advocacy aims to address legal and regulatory barriers that may impede the return and reintegration of diaspora members.

Collaborating with government agencies, legal experts, and international organizations, advocacy seeks to streamline processes and provide necessary support.

8. Cultural Exchange Programs:

Advocacy encourages cultural exchange programs that facilitate a deeper understanding between returning diaspora members and local communities.

These programs contribute to building bridges, fostering mutual respect, and promoting social cohesion.

9. Mentorship and Support Networks:

Advocacy supports the establishment of mentorship programs and support networks for returnees.

These networks provide guidance, resources, and a sense of community, easing the transition and promoting successful reintegration.

10. Recognition of Overseas Education and Experience:

Advocacy emphasizes the recognition of overseas education and professional experience, ensuring that returnees' qualifications are valued and utilized.

This recognition contributes to the effective utilization of skills brought back by the diaspora.

11. Healthcare Access for Returnees:

Advocacy efforts target improved access to healthcare services for returnees, recognizing the importance of health in successful reintegration.

Collaborating with healthcare institutions, advocacy aims to address potential barriers to healthcare access.

12. Housing and Infrastructure Support:

Advocacy focuses on policies and initiatives that provide housing and infrastructure support for returnees.

Adequate housing and infrastructure contribute to a comfortable and supportive environment for returning diaspora members.

13. Community Integration Programs:

Advocacy supports community integration programs that facilitate the active participation of returnees in local community activities.

These programs promote social inclusion and help create a sense of belonging.

14. Recognition of Diaspora Expertise:

Advocacy emphasizes the recognition and utilization of diaspora expertise in national development plans.

Engaging returnees in decision-making processes ensures that their skills are effectively leveraged for the benefit of Eritrea.

Through these advocacy efforts, the goal is to create an environment that encourages the return of the diaspora, recognizes their contributions, and supports a smooth and successful reintegration process, ultimately contributing to the holistic development of Eritrea.

Balancing Activism and Diplomacy:

The Eritrean diaspora, passionate about contributing to positive change in their homeland, navigates the delicate balance between activism and diplomacy. This delicate equilibrium is essential for effectively advocating for human rights, democratic governance, and socio-economic development in Eritrea while maintaining constructive relationships with international stakeholders.

1. Advocacy for Human Rights:

Activism involves robust advocacy for human rights, highlighting issues such as political repression, freedom of expression, and the rights of refugees.

Diplomacy complements activism by engaging with international organizations to address human rights concerns through constructive dialogue and collaboration.

2. Engaging with International Institutions:

Activism includes grassroots movements, awareness campaigns, and public demonstrations to draw attention to the challenges faced by Eritreans.

Diplomacy focuses on engaging with international institutions, governments, and diplomatic missions to garner support, build alliances, and influence policies for positive change.

3. Grassroots Activism and Community Building:

Activism at the grassroots level involves community building, organizing events, and fostering a sense of unity within the diaspora.

Diplomacy extends to engaging diaspora communities in constructive dialogue, building consensus, and aligning collective efforts with diplomatic strategies for a unified approach.

4. Advocacy for Democratic Governance:

Activism advocates for democratic governance, transparency, and the rule of law within Eritrea.

Diplomacy involves dialogue with international partners to promote democratic values, encouraging diplomatic efforts that support governance reforms.

5. Media Engagement and Public Relations:

Activism utilizes media engagement, social media campaigns, and public relations to raise awareness and mobilize support.

Diplomacy focuses on strategic communication, presenting a positive image of Eritrea, and engaging with international media to shape narratives constructively.

6. Collaborative Initiatives with NGOs:

Activism involves collaborations with non-governmental organizations (NGOs) to address humanitarian, human rights, and development issues.

Diplomacy extends to engaging with international NGOs, facilitating partnerships, and ensuring coordinated efforts for maximum impact.

7. Advocacy for Policy Change:

Activism strives for policy change through public pressure, petitions, and grassroots movements.

Diplomacy involves engaging with policymakers, participating in international forums, and influencing policy discussions to create an enabling environment for positive change.

8. Cultural Diplomacy and Heritage Preservation:

Activism includes efforts to preserve Eritrean cultural heritage, promote diversity, and celebrate the unique identity of Eritreans.

Diplomacy involves cultural diplomacy initiatives, engaging with international cultural organizations, and showcasing Eritrea's rich heritage to foster understanding and appreciation.

9. Humanitarian Aid and Relief Efforts:

Activism leads to direct involvement in humanitarian aid and relief efforts, responding to immediate needs and crises.

Diplomacy complements this by engaging with international institutions to advocate for sustained humanitarian assistance and policies that address the root causes of crises.

10. Collaboration with Diplomatic Missions:

Activism includes engaging with diplomatic missions to raise awareness about Eritrean issues and seek international support.

Diplomacy involves fostering positive relationships with diplomatic missions, facilitating dialogue, and exploring avenues for collaboration on common goals.

11. Advocacy for Social and Economic Development:

Activism advocates for social and economic development within Eritrea through grassroots initiatives and community-led projects.

Diplomacy involves engaging with international partners, promoting investment, and advocating for policies that support sustainable development.

12. Participation in International Forums:

Activism includes participation in international forums to present Eritrean perspectives and advocate for change.

Diplomacy focuses on effective representation, networking, and influencing global discussions to shape policies that align with the aspirations of Eritreans.

13. Mediating Disputes and Building Bridges:

Activism involves mediating disputes within the diaspora and building bridges between diverse perspectives.

Diplomacy extends to mediating international disputes, fostering diplomatic solutions, and building relationships to address regional challenges.

14. Public-Private Partnerships for Development:

Activism includes promoting public-private partnerships to drive economic development.

Diplomacy involves engaging with international businesses, fostering investment, and creating an environment conducive to sustainable economic growth.

Balancing activism and diplomacy requires a nuanced and strategic approach, acknowledging the strengths of both while ensuring a cohesive and effective advocacy for positive change in

Eritrea. This delicate balance enables the diaspora to navigate challenges, foster collaboration, and contribute to the holistic development of their homeland.

Chapter Seven

The Failures of Dictatorship

In the intricate tapestry of Eritrean history, one thread stands out starkly—the era marked by authoritarian rule. This chapter explores the failures of dictatorship, unraveling the impact on governance, society, and the dreams of a nation.

7.1 The Grip of Authoritarianism:

Delving into the mechanisms of authoritarian rule, this section illuminates the centralization of power, suppression of dissent, and erosion of democratic institutions.

Examining how authoritarianism stifles political pluralism and undermines the principles of governance.

7.2 Repression and Human Rights Violations:

Unmasking the human toll of dictatorship, this section exposes the systematic repression, arbitrary detentions, and violations of basic human rights.

Stories of individuals and communities grappling with the consequences of living under a regime that prioritizes control over compassion.

7.3 Economic Conundrums:

Analyzing the economic mismanagement and challenges arising from authoritarian governance.

The impact on economic growth, foreign investments, and the livelihoods of ordinary citizens struggling in the face of fiscal policies that prioritize regime survival.

7.4 Erosion of Social Fabric:

Investigating how dictatorship corrodes the social fabric, creating divisions and fostering an atmosphere of fear.

Stories of communities grappling with the breakdown of trust and the challenges of rebuilding social cohesion in the aftermath.

7.5 Strained International Relations:

Exploring the strain imposed on Eritrea's international relations due to the actions of the authoritarian regime.

The diplomatic isolation, sanctions, and challenges in fostering collaborative relationships with the global community.

7.6 The Refugee Crisis:

Unraveling the complex web of factors that contribute to the mass exodus of Eritreans seeking refuge abroad.

Examining the plight of refugees and the global implications of a nation forced to export its people due to political persecution and economic hardship.

7.7 Environmental Degradation:

Investigating the environmental impact of authoritarian rule, including policies that neglect conservation and sustainable practices.

The consequences of unchecked exploitation of natural resources and the urgent need for environmental stewardship.

7.8 Stifling Intellectual and Artistic Expression:

Examining the constraints placed on intellectual and artistic expression under authoritarian rule.

Stories of writers, artists, and thinkers navigating censorship, self-censorship, and the suppression of free thought.

7.9 Education in Crisis:

Analyzing the challenges faced by the education system under authoritarian governance.

The erosion of academic freedom, limitations on critical thinking, and the impact on the intellectual development of future generations.

7.10 The Generational Divide:

Exploring the generational dynamics influenced by dictatorship.

The experiences of older generations who witnessed the struggle for independence and the aspirations of the youth grappling with the failures of the current political landscape.

7.11 Resistance and Resilience:

Highlighting instances of resistance and resilience against authoritarian rule.

Stories of individuals and groups who, despite facing adversity, continue to advocate for change, justice, and a more inclusive future.

7.12 International Responses and Interventions:

Examining the responses of the international community to the failures of dictatorship in Eritrea.

The role of diplomatic pressures, sanctions, and humanitarian interventions in addressing the challenges faced by the Eritrean people.

7.13 Voices of Dissent from Within:

Amplifying the voices of dissent within Eritrea, showcasing the courage of those who speak out against the failures of dictatorship.

The challenges and risks faced by activists, journalists, and ordinary citizens who dare to question the status quo.

7.14 Pathways to a Democratic Future:

Exploring potential pathways toward a democratic future for Eritrea.

The role of internal and external actors in fostering a transition to a governance system that prioritizes inclusivity, human rights, and sustainable development.

In unraveling the failures of dictatorship, this chapter aims to shine a light on the resilience of the Eritrean people and the collective pursuit of a future marked by democracy, justice, and prosperity.

7.1 The Grip of Authoritarianism

Centralization of Power:

In the heart of Eritrea's recent history lies the formidable grip of authoritarianism, where power became concentrated in the hands of a few. The centralized authority, exemplified by the ruling regime, suppressed the development of democratic institutions, stifling the diverse voices that form the tapestry of Eritrean society. Decisions made in the echelons of power resonated without meaningful consultation, leaving a void in the participatory governance that is essential for a thriving nation.

Suppression of Dissent:

Authoritarian rule in Eritrea manifested through the harsh suppression of dissent. Political opposition was met with severe consequences, including arbitrary arrests, imprisonment without due process, and a climate of fear that permeated communities. Dissenters faced not only legal repercussions but also social ostracization, creating an environment where expressing alternative views became perilous.

Erosion of Democratic Institutions:

The foundations of a robust democracy crumbled under the weight of authoritarianism. Institutions meant to uphold democratic values, such as a free press, an independent judiciary, and representative governance, faced erosion. The regime's consolidation of power resulted in a governance system that favored control over transparency, leaving citizens with limited avenues for expressing their aspirations and concerns.

Limitations on Political Pluralism:

Authoritarian governance in Eritrea stifled political pluralism, leaving little room for diverse political ideologies to coexist. Opposition parties faced suppression, hindering the development of a vibrant political landscape. The absence of political pluralism not only undermined democratic principles but also impeded the ability to address the complex challenges facing the nation through inclusive and varied perspectives.

Challenges to Democratic Transition:

The grip of authoritarianism presents significant challenges to any democratic transition. Transitioning from centralized rule to a more participatory and inclusive system requires dismantling deeply entrenched power structures and fostering an environment where diverse voices can contribute to the nation's future. Navigating this transition demands resilience, strategic planning, and a commitment to democratic values.

As Eritreans grapple with the consequences of authoritarian rule, the journey toward a more democratic future necessitates a collective effort to rebuild democratic institutions, nurture political pluralism, and ensure that the governance of the nation reflects the diverse aspirations of its people. This chapter explores the multifaceted impact of authoritarianism, shedding light on both its immediate consequences and the long-term challenges it poses to the democratic aspirations of Eritrea.

7.2 Repression and Human Rights Violations

Systematic Repression:

Under the shadow of authoritarian rule in Eritrea, a dark chapter unfolded marked by systematic repression. The regime's mechanisms of control extended to all facets of life, instilling fear and suppressing dissent. Citizens faced restrictions on freedom of expression, assembly, and association, leading to a climate of pervasive fear and self-censorship.

Arbitrary Detentions and Forced Disappearances:

The regime's grip on power manifested through arbitrary detentions and forced disappearances.

Individuals expressing dissenting opinions, whether political activists, journalists, or ordinary citizens, found themselves subjected to imprisonment without due process. Families were left in agonizing uncertainty, unsure of the fate and whereabouts of their loved ones.

Violations of Basic Human Rights:

Basic human rights were systematically violated, with reports of torture, inhumane treatment, and denial of fundamental freedoms. The right to a fair trial was undermined, as individuals faced prolonged detention without access to legal representation. This pattern of abuse not only violated international human rights norms but also left a lasting scar on the fabric of Eritrean society.

Erosion of Freedom of the Press:

The regime's control extended to the realm of media, resulting in the erosion of freedom of the press. Independent journalism became a rare commodity as the government stifled dissenting voices, shuttering independent media outlets and leaving citizens with limited access to diverse perspectives. Journalists faced persecution, forcing many into exile to escape the heavy hand of censorship.

Impact on Civil Society:

The repressive environment had a chilling effect on civil society, limiting the ability of citizens to organize, advocate, and express their concerns. Non-governmental organizations faced severe restrictions, hindering their capacity to address pressing issues and contribute to positive social change. The erosion of civil society spaces left a void in the collective voice of the people.

Strained Social Cohesion:

Human rights violations strained the social fabric of Eritrean society. Families were torn apart by forced conscriptions, arbitrary detentions, and the loss of loved ones. Communities lived in perpetual fear, hesitant to openly discuss their grievances. The erosion of trust and social cohesion became a consequence of the regime's repressive tactics.

International Outcry and Calls for Accountability:

The human rights violations in Eritrea did not go unnoticed on the international stage. Advocacy groups, human rights organizations, and the global community raised their voices in condemnation. Calls for accountability echoed through international forums, urging the regime to address the egregious human rights abuses and engage in meaningful reforms.

Refugees Fleeing Repression:

The intensity of repression drove a significant number of Eritreans to seek refuge abroad. Fleeing the dire human rights situation, many embarked on perilous journeys, becoming part of the global refugee crisis. The experiences of Eritrean refugees underscored the urgency of addressing the root causes of repression and creating conditions for a safe and dignified return.

A Call for Justice and Healing:

In the face of repression and human rights violations, a collective call for justice and healing emerged. Eritreans, both within the country and abroad, advocated for accountability, the release of political prisoners, and the establishment of mechanisms to address past wrongs. The quest for justice became intertwined with the broader struggle for a democratic and inclusive future.

As Eritreans confront the legacy of repression and human rights violations, the journey toward healing and justice becomes a critical component of the nation's path forward. This chapter explores the profound impact of repression on individuals and society, shedding light on the resilience of those who continue to seek justice, accountability, and a brighter future for Eritrea.

7.4 Erosion of Social Fabric

Trust Deficit and Community Distrust:

The grip of authoritarianism in Eritrea has inflicted profound wounds on the social fabric of the nation, leading to a trust deficit and widespread community distrust. The erosion of trust is not only evident in interpersonal relationships but extends to institutions, including those traditionally relied upon for support and justice. Suspicion and fear permeate interactions, hindering the natural bonds that hold communities together.

Disintegration of Communal Bonds:

Authoritarian rule has contributed to the disintegration of communal bonds that once formed the backbone of Eritrean society. The bonds between neighbors, friends, and extended families have been strained as individuals navigate a landscape where expressing dissent or holding divergent opinions may lead to ostracization. The communal spaces that traditionally fostered unity and collaboration have been eroded.

Familial Strains and Separation:

The policy of indefinite national service and the forced conscription of citizens have strained familial ties to the breaking point. Families find themselves torn apart, with loved ones forcibly separated for extended periods. The emotional toll of not knowing the fate of family members, coupled with the economic hardships imposed by the regime, has contributed to a fractured familial landscape.

Impacts on Mental Health:

The erosion of the social fabric has had severe implications for the mental health of individuals and communities. The constant atmosphere of fear, the uncertainty surrounding the fate of detained family members, and the restrictions on free expression have led to increased stress, anxiety, and trauma. Mental health challenges are not only personal but also societal, affecting the overall well-being of the population.

Suppression of Cultural Expressions:

Authoritarian rule in Eritrea has extended its reach to the suppression of cultural expressions. The vibrant tapestry of Eritrean culture, which once served as a unifying force, has been stifled. Artists, musicians, and writers face constraints on their creativity, and cultural events are subject to strict scrutiny. The suppression of cultural diversity contributes to a sense of homogeneity that further erodes the richness of Eritrea's social tapestry.

Impact on Interpersonal Relationships:

The pervasive climate of fear and self-censorship has infiltrated interpersonal relationships, stifling open and honest communication. Friends and family members may hesitate to discuss political issues or express dissenting opinions, leading to a culture of guarded interactions. The erosion of trust has made it challenging for individuals to navigate relationships with the freedom and openness that characterize healthy societies.

Challenges in Rebuilding Social Cohesion:

Rebuilding the social fabric of Eritrea poses significant challenges in the aftermath of authoritarian rule. Addressing the distrust, strained relationships, and communal divisions requires intentional efforts to create spaces for dialogue, healing, and reconciliation. Communities must navigate a path toward rebuilding trust and fostering a sense of unity that transcends the scars of the past.

Resilience and Community Initiatives:

Amidst the challenges, stories of resilience and community initiatives emerge. Grassroots efforts to strengthen social bonds, support mental health, and revitalize cultural expressions signify the indomitable spirit of the Eritrean people. Whether through community gatherings, cultural events, or mutual support networks, individuals strive to reclaim and rebuild the social fabric that defines their collective identity.

As Eritreans confront the erosion of their social fabric, the journey toward healing and rebuilding becomes an integral part of the broader quest for a democratic, inclusive, and socially cohesive future. This chapter delves into the intricate dynamics of social erosion and the resilient efforts to weave a new narrative of unity and community strength.

7.5 Strained International Relations

Diplomatic Isolation:

The grip of authoritarianism in Eritrea has resulted in strained international relations, marked by diplomatic isolation. The government's actions, including human rights abuses, suppression of dissent, and strained regional relationships, have led to a diminution of Eritrea's standing on the global stage. International diplomatic circles have responded with condemnation, resulting in Eritrea's isolation from collaborative diplomatic efforts.

Sanctions and Global Condemnation:

Eritrea's actions under authoritarian rule have triggered international sanctions and widespread condemnation. The global community, including the United Nations, has expressed concerns over human rights violations, contributing to a diplomatic climate that places Eritrea under scrutiny. Sanctions, both economic and political, underscore the international community's commitment to holding the regime accountable for its actions.

Regional Tensions:

Authoritarian governance in Eritrea has contributed to regional tensions, particularly in the Horn of Africa. Historical disputes with neighboring countries, coupled with the Eritrean government's policies and actions, have led to a complex geopolitical landscape. Strained regional relations have not only isolated Eritrea but also contributed to broader instability in the region.

Impacts on Trade and Development:

Diplomatic isolation has tangible consequences for Eritrea's economic landscape. The strained international relations impede trade, economic cooperation, and foreign investment. The nation's development is hindered by a lack of collaborative efforts and partnerships that could contribute to sustainable growth. The repercussions are felt not only by the government but also by the population striving for economic stability.

Humanitarian Consequences:

Strained international relations exacerbate humanitarian challenges in Eritrea. Limited diplomatic engagement can impede the flow of international aid, leaving vulnerable populations without essential resources. The consequences are particularly severe in times of crises, such as natural disasters or health emergencies, where international cooperation is crucial for effective response and recovery.

Refugee Crisis and Regional Impact:

The authoritarian governance in Eritrea has contributed significantly to the global refugee crisis. The strained international relations, combined with internal challenges, have forced many Eritreans to flee their homeland. The resulting diaspora and refugee crisis not only impact Eritreans but also place a burden on neighboring countries and the international community as a whole.

Opportunities for Diplomatic Engagement:

While the international community has expressed condemnation, there are opportunities for diplomatic engagement and dialogue. Efforts to encourage positive reforms, uphold human rights, and address regional tensions could pave the way for improved relations. Diplomatic initiatives that prioritize dialogue and collaboration may contribute to easing tensions and fostering a more constructive relationship with the global community.

Civil Society and Diaspora Engagement:

Civil society and diaspora engagement play a crucial role in navigating strained international relations. Eritrean diaspora communities, with their global reach and influence, can serve as bridges for international understanding. Civil society organizations advocating for positive change and human rights contribute to reshaping international perceptions and building alliances with global partners.

Aspirations for Reintegration:

Despite diplomatic challenges, there are aspirations for reintegration into the international community. A commitment to democratic reforms, human rights, and regional stability could open avenues for renewed diplomatic relationships. The people of Eritrea, both within the country and abroad, yearn for a future where the nation actively engages with the world in a spirit of cooperation and mutual benefit.

As Eritrea grapples with strained international relations, the possibilities for a more positive diplomatic future rest on a commitment to democratic governance, respect for human rights, and collaborative efforts to address regional challenges. This chapter explores the complexities of Eritrea's diplomatic landscape and the potential pathways toward a more constructive engagement with the global community.

7.6 The Refugee Crisis

Forced Displacement and Flight:

The authoritarian governance in Eritrea has played a central role in generating a significant refugee crisis, with Eritreans compelled to flee their homeland. Forced conscription, human rights abuses, and economic hardship have driven many to embark on perilous journeys in search of safety and a better life. The refugee crisis, emblematic of the struggles faced by Eritreans, has profound implications on a global scale.

Humanitarian Challenges on the Journey:

Eritrean refugees undertaking the journey face a myriad of humanitarian challenges. Crossing borders under precarious conditions, navigating harsh terrains, and relying on informal networks for support, refugees endure physical and emotional hardships. The journey to seek refuge often exposes them to exploitation, violence, and the uncertainties of an uncertain future.

Global Displacement and Diaspora:

The Eritrean refugee crisis has contributed to the global displacement phenomenon, with Eritreans forming a substantial diaspora community worldwide. The diaspora, scattered across various countries, reflects the diverse experiences of displacement. These communities, while contributing significantly to their host nations, yearn for a resolution to the issues that forced them to leave their homeland.

Challenges in Host Countries:

Host countries receiving Eritrean refugees face their own set of challenges. Strained resources, cultural integration, and the need for adequate infrastructure to support the influx of newcomers create complex scenarios. The resilience of host communities and their ability to provide support to refugees influence the success of integration efforts and the overall well-being of displaced populations.

Trauma and Mental Health Impacts:

The refugee crisis has profound mental health implications for displaced Eritreans. Trauma resulting from the experiences in Eritrea, coupled with the challenges of displacement and resettlement, contributes to mental health issues. Addressing the mental health needs of Eritrean refugees requires comprehensive support systems and a recognition of the unique challenges they face.

Family Separation and Its Toll:

Many Eritrean refugees experience family separation, adding an emotional toll to their journey. The forced dispersal of families, often due to one or more family members being unable to escape together, creates a profound sense of loss and longing. The impact of family separation resonates not only in the emotional well-being of individuals but also in the dynamics of the diaspora.

Contributions of the Diaspora:

Despite the challenges, the Eritrean diaspora has made significant contributions to their host countries. From academics and professionals to artists and entrepreneurs, the diaspora showcases the resilience, diversity, and potential of the Eritrean people. While thriving in their adopted homes, members of the diaspora remain deeply connected to the vision of a better Eritrea.

Calls for Resolution and Repatriation:

Eritreans in the diaspora, as well as those within the country, yearn for a resolution to the refugee crisis and the conditions that led to displacement. Calls for repatriation echo the desire to return to a stable and democratic Eritrea, where human rights are upheld, and individuals can rebuild their lives without fear of persecution.

International Responses and Humanitarian Aid:

The international community plays a crucial role in responding to the Eritrean refugee crisis. Humanitarian aid, support for host countries, and diplomatic efforts aimed at addressing the root causes of displacement are essential components. Collaborative international responses are needed to create conditions conducive to the voluntary return and sustainable reintegration of refugees.

The Role of Civil Society:

Civil society organizations, both within and outside Eritrea, play a pivotal role in addressing the refugee crisis. Advocacy for human rights, providing support to refugees, and fostering dialogue on potential solutions are key functions. The collective efforts of civil society contribute to a comprehensive approach to addressing the challenges faced by Eritrean refugees.

The refugee crisis is a poignant chapter in the story of Eritrea, highlighting the resilience of those forced to flee, the challenges faced by host communities, and the collective aspirations for a resolution that allows for the dignified return and rebuilding of lives in a transformed and inclusive Eritrea.

7.8 Stifling Intellectual and Artistic Expression

Censorship and Self-Censorship:

Under authoritarian rule in Eritrea, intellectual and artistic expression has faced stifling censorship. The government's control extends to media outlets, publications, and artistic works, limiting the freedom of expression. The pervasive climate of fear has led to self-censorship among writers, journalists, artists, and intellectuals who fear reprisals for expressing dissenting views or challenging the status quo.

Constraints on Literature and Journalism:

The literary and journalistic landscape in Eritrea has been profoundly affected by authoritarian rule. Writers and journalists navigate a narrow path, adhering to prescribed narratives and avoiding topics deemed sensitive by the government. Independent publications face suppression, resulting in a scarcity of diverse voices and perspectives within Eritrean literature and journalism.

Impact on Artistic Creativity:

Artistic creativity in Eritrea has faced constraints imposed by the regime. Musicians, visual artists, and performers operate within the boundaries set by the government, with expressions of dissent or criticism subject to censorship. The vibrant cultural scene that once thrived faces limitations, hindering the exploration of diverse themes and perspectives.

The Role of Education:

Educational institutions, meant to be hubs of intellectual exploration, have also experienced stifling constraints. Academic freedom is curtailed as educators and students face limitations on the subjects they can engage with and the perspectives they can explore. The suppression of intellectual discourse within educational settings hampers the development of critical thinking and diverse viewpoints.

Impact on Dissenting Voices:

Dissenting voices, whether within academia, the arts, or intellectual circles, face severe consequences. Scholars, writers, and artists who dare to challenge the authoritarian regime risk imprisonment, harassment, and exile. The suppression of dissenting voices not only curtails individual freedoms but also stifles the vibrancy of intellectual and artistic discourse within Eritrea.

Exile and Diaspora Voices:

Many intellectuals, writers, and artists have chosen exile as a means of preserving their ability to express themselves freely. The Eritrean diaspora becomes a vital space for those who continue their intellectual and artistic pursuits without fear of reprisals. Exiled voices contribute to a global narrative on Eritrea, shedding light on the realities faced within the country.

Digital Spaces and Surveillance:

The rise of digital spaces has provided an alternative platform for expression, albeit under the watchful eye of government surveillance. Online platforms become spaces for Eritreans to share their perspectives, but the fear of repercussions persists. The regime's surveillance apparatus extends into the digital realm, impacting the ability of individuals to engage in open discourse.

Creative Resilience and Subversive Art:

Despite the constraints, Eritrean intellectuals and artists demonstrate remarkable resilience through creative subversion. Through coded messages, symbolic expressions, and alternative narratives, individuals find ways to convey dissent and critique. Subversive art becomes a form of resistance, challenging the imposed limitations and providing a glimpse into the resilience of Eritrean creativity.

Diaspora Initiatives for Cultural Preservation:

In the diaspora, initiatives emerge to preserve and celebrate Eritrean culture and intellectual heritage. Cultural events, artistic exhibitions, and intellectual forums in diaspora communities become vital spaces for fostering creativity, reclaiming narratives, and sustaining the rich cultural tapestry that authoritarian rule seeks to suppress.

International Solidarity and Advocacy:

International solidarity plays a crucial role in supporting Eritrean intellectuals and artists. Advocacy efforts highlight the importance of freedom of expression, artistic freedom, and intellectual exploration. Global networks become platforms for amplifying suppressed voices and advocating for the protection of intellectual and artistic rights.

In exploring the stifling of intellectual and artistic expression under authoritarian rule, this chapter delves into the complex landscape faced by Eritrean writers, artists, and intellectuals. It examines the impact on diverse creative pursuits, the resilience demonstrated in the face of constraints, and the role of the diaspora in preserving and advancing Eritrea's intellectual and artistic heritage.

7.9 Education in Crisis

Suppression of Academic Freedom:

Authoritarian rule in Eritrea has cast a long shadow over the education system, leading to the suppression of academic freedom. Educators, scholars, and students find themselves navigating a restrictive environment where certain topics are deemed off-limits, and critical discussions may lead to repercussions. The erosion of academic freedom stifles the intellectual vibrancy that is essential for educational institutions.

Censorship of Curriculum and Textbooks:

The government's control extends to the content taught in schools, resulting in the censorship of curriculum and textbooks. Certain historical events, political ideologies, and perspectives are deliberately omitted or distorted. The shaping of young minds is influenced by a narrow narrative that aligns with the regime's agenda, limiting the ability of students to engage with diverse viewpoints.

Policing of Thought and Expression:

Educational institutions become spaces where the policing of thought and expression is prevalent. Students and educators face the constant scrutiny of their words and actions, creating an atmosphere of self-censorship. The fear of reprisals for expressing dissenting views or engaging in critical discussions stifles the free exchange of ideas that is fundamental to the educational process.

Impact on Critical Thinking:

The erosion of academic freedom and the censorship of educational content directly impact the development of critical thinking skills. Students are discouraged from questioning authority, analyzing multiple perspectives, and engaging in independent thought. The result is an educational landscape where conformity is prioritized over intellectual curiosity, hindering the cultivation of a generation of critical thinkers.

Disruption of Academic Pursuits:

Forced conscription and the indefinite national service policy disrupt the academic pursuits of many young Eritreans. Students are conscripted into military service at a young age, diverting them from their educational trajectories. The interruption in academic pursuits contributes to a loss of educational opportunities and undermines the potential for personal and national development.

Brain Drain and Loss of Intellectual Capital:

The suppression of academic freedom and the challenges faced by the education system contribute to a significant brain drain. Eritrea loses a wealth of intellectual capital as scholars, educators, and students seek opportunities abroad. The exodus of intellectual resources hampers the nation's ability to address complex challenges and impedes progress in various fields.

Struggle for Access to Education:

Access to education becomes a significant challenge, particularly for marginalized communities and those in remote areas. Limited resources, infrastructural challenges, and the prioritization of certain regions over others create disparities in educational opportunities. The struggle for access to quality education exacerbates existing inequalities within Eritrean society.

Impact on Future Generations:

The crisis in education has profound implications for future generations in Eritrea. The curtailed development of critical thinking, limited access to diverse perspectives, and disruptions in academic pursuits hinder the ability of young Eritreans to contribute meaningfully to the nation's progress. The cyclical nature of the crisis perpetuates a cycle of educational challenges that affect successive generations.

Diaspora Initiatives for Educational Support:

In the diaspora, initiatives emerge to support education in Eritrea. Diaspora communities recognize the importance of preserving educational opportunities for the next generation and work to provide resources, scholarships, and mentorship programs. These initiatives aim to counteract the challenges faced by the education system within the country.

International Efforts for Educational Development:

International organizations and advocacy groups contribute to efforts aimed at addressing the educational crisis in Eritrea. Initiatives focused on improving access to education, advocating for academic freedom, and supporting the development of a robust and inclusive education system become integral components of global efforts to uplift the educational landscape in Eritrea.

Exploring the crisis in education under authoritarian rule, this chapter delves into the multifaceted challenges faced by Eritrean students, educators, and the broader educational system. It examines the impact on critical thinking, access to education, and the initiatives undertaken by diaspora communities and the international community to support educational development in Eritrea.

Chapter Eight

Toward a Better Future

8.1 The Call for Democratic Reforms:

Amidst the challenges, a resounding call for democratic reforms echoes across Eritrea. Citizens, intellectuals, and activists within the country, as well as the diaspora, unite in their aspirations for a future defined by democratic governance, respect for human rights, and the rule of law. The vision for a better Eritrea centers on dismantling authoritarian structures and establishing a participatory system that reflects the diverse aspirations of its people.

8.2 The Role of Civil Society:

Civil society emerges as a driving force in the quest for a better future. Advocacy groups, human rights organizations, and community initiatives play a crucial role in raising awareness, documenting human rights abuses, and fostering dialogue. The resilience of civil society becomes instrumental in challenging authoritarianism and laying the groundwork for a more inclusive and democratic Eritrea.

8.3 International Solidarity:

The global community stands in solidarity with the people of Eritrea, advocating for positive change and supporting efforts toward democratic reforms. International organizations, governments, and grassroots movements contribute to diplomatic pressure, human rights advocacy, and initiatives aimed at addressing the root causes of challenges faced by Eritreans.

8.4 Rebuilding Democratic Institutions:

The journey toward a better future involves the rebuilding of democratic institutions that have been eroded under authoritarian rule. Establishing transparent governance structures, nurturing a free press, and fostering political pluralism become paramount. The reconstruction of democratic institutions forms the foundation for a system that upholds the values of justice, accountability, and civic participation.

8.5 Empowering Communities:

Empowering communities becomes a focal point in the pursuit of positive change. Grassroots initiatives, community engagement, and capacity-building efforts contribute to the resilience of individuals and communities. By fostering a sense of agency and participation, communities become active contributors to the transformation of Eritrean society.

8.6 Truth and Reconciliation:

Addressing the wounds of the past and promoting national healing become integral to the journey toward a better future. Truth and reconciliation processes, both within the country and in the diaspora, provide spaces for acknowledging historical injustices, documenting human rights violations, and fostering dialogue. The pursuit of truth becomes a catalyst for reconciliation and unity.

8.7 Economic Development and Social Justice:

Economic development is envisioned as a catalyst for social justice and inclusive growth. Sustainable development initiatives, job creation, and investments in education and healthcare contribute to the well-being of the population. The vision for a better future prioritizes economic policies that uplift communities, reduce inequality, and foster a resilient and self-reliant nation.

8.8 Diaspora Engagement and Return:

The Eritrean diaspora plays a pivotal role in shaping the nation's future. Diaspora communities actively engage in initiatives that support education, healthcare, and economic development within the country. As conditions improve, the possibility of diaspora members returning to contribute their skills, knowledge, and resources to the rebuilding of Eritrea becomes a tangible prospect.

8.9 Cultural Renaissance and Intellectual Freedom:

A cultural renaissance unfolds as artistic expression, literature, and intellectual discourse flourish in an atmosphere of freedom and creativity. The lifting of constraints on intellectual and artistic freedom allows for a vibrant exchange of ideas, the exploration of diverse perspectives, and the celebration of Eritrea's rich cultural heritage.

8.10 International Collaboration for Sustainable Development:

International collaboration becomes a cornerstone of Eritrea's journey toward a better future. Collaborative efforts with the global community, regional partners, and international organizations contribute to sustainable development, peacebuilding, and the realization of a vision where Eritrea stands as a beacon of democracy, human rights, and prosperity.

As Eritrea charts its course toward a better future, the collective efforts of its people, civil society, the diaspora, and the international community converge in a shared vision of a nation defined by democratic values, justice, and inclusive development. This chapter explores the multifaceted pathways leading to a brighter tomorrow for Eritrea.

8.1 The Call for Democratic Reforms

A Unified Voice:

The call for democratic reforms reverberates across Eritrea, uniting the voices of citizens yearning for a future marked by freedom, justice, and participatory governance. In town squares, community gatherings, and online forums, a unified chorus emerges—a collective demand for an end to authoritarian rule and the establishment of democratic institutions that reflect the diverse aspirations of the Eritrean people.

Grassroots Movements:

At the heart of the call for democratic reforms are grassroots movements led by activists, intellectuals, and ordinary citizens. These movements, driven by a shared commitment to democracy, human rights, and the rule of law, become catalysts for change. Through peaceful protests, advocacy campaigns, and community dialogues, they galvanize support and inspire hope for a more inclusive and representative political landscape.

Demands for Political Pluralism:

Central to the call for democratic reforms is the demand for political pluralism. Eritreans envision a political environment where multiple parties can freely participate, allowing for a diversity of ideas and perspectives. The quest for political pluralism reflects a commitment to dismantling the monopoly of power and fostering a system that genuinely represents the will of the people.

Inclusive Constitutional Process:

The call for democratic reforms extends to the need for an inclusive and participatory constitutional process. Eritreans advocate for a constitution that safeguards fundamental rights, guarantees the separation of powers, and establishes mechanisms for transparent and accountable governance. The drafting of a new constitution becomes a collective endeavor that engages citizens from all walks of life.

Human Rights and Rule of Law:

Fundamental to the call for democratic reforms is a steadfast commitment to human rights and the rule of law. Eritreans envision a future where citizens are protected by a legal framework that upholds their dignity, freedom of expression, and right to dissent. The establishment of independent judiciary systems becomes a cornerstone in ensuring accountability and justice.

Empowering Civil Society:

The call for democratic reforms places a strong emphasis on empowering civil society. Advocacy groups, human rights organizations, and community initiatives become vital actors in holding the government accountable and promoting democratic values. As civil society thrives, it serves as a watchdog, amplifying the voices of the people and contributing to the checks and balances essential for a vibrant democracy.

International Support for Democratic Transitions:

Eritreans appealing for democratic reforms seek support from the international community. They call upon governments, international organizations, and the global civil society to stand in solidarity and assist in the transition to democracy. International support is seen as a crucial factor in providing the necessary resources, expertise, and diplomatic pressure to facilitate a smooth and sustainable transition.

Dialogue and Reconciliation:

The call for democratic reforms is accompanied by a commitment to national dialogue and reconciliation. Eritreans recognize the importance of healing the wounds of the past, fostering understanding among diverse communities, and building a shared vision for the future. In the spirit of unity, dialogue becomes a tool for reconciliation and nation-building.

Youth Engagement:

The call for democratic reforms resonates strongly among the youth—a demographic eager to shape the future of Eritrea. Youth-led initiatives, activism, and civic engagement become instrumental in driving the demand for democratic change. The energy and vision of the youth inject dynamism into the movement, emphasizing the intergenerational commitment to a democratic Eritrea.

As Eritrea responds to the call for democratic reforms, this chapter explores the multifaceted nature of the movement, examining the motivations, strategies, and aspirations that propel the nation toward a future grounded in democratic principles and the collective will of its people.

8.2 The Role of Civil Society

Advocacy for Democratic Values:

In the pursuit of democratic reforms, civil society emerges as a powerful force advocating for democratic values, human rights, and the rule of law. Organizations dedicated to the promotion of democracy become essential voices, leveraging their platforms to raise awareness, mobilize citizens, and demand accountability from the government.

Watchdogs for Accountability:

Civil society organizations transform into watchdogs, closely monitoring government actions and policies. Through meticulous documentation of human rights abuses, electoral processes, and governance practices, these organizations play a crucial role in holding those in power accountable. Their efforts serve as a check on authoritarian tendencies, contributing to the establishment of transparent and accountable governance.

Civic Education Initiatives:

Recognizing the importance of an informed citizenry, civil society spearheads civic education initiatives. Workshops, seminars, and community outreach programs aim to empower citizens with knowledge about their rights, the democratic process, and the role they play in shaping the future of the nation. Civic education becomes a cornerstone in building an engaged and politically aware populace.

Bridge Builders and Mediators:

Amidst calls for dialogue and reconciliation, civil society organizations assume the role of bridge builders and mediators. They facilitate conversations between diverse communities, fostering understanding and creating spaces for constructive dialogue. By acting as intermediaries, civil society contributes to the resolution of conflicts, the mending of social divisions, and the forging of a shared national identity.

Human Rights Defenders:

In an environment where human rights are often compromised, civil society organizations become champions of human rights. Human rights defenders within civil society work tirelessly to shed light on abuses, provide support to victims, and advocate for systemic changes. Their resilience in the face of adversity demonstrates the unwavering commitment to the protection of basic freedoms.

Grassroots Mobilization:

Civil society organizations excel in grassroots mobilization, galvanizing communities and individuals to actively participate in the democratic reform movement. Through community organizing, awareness campaigns, and public demonstrations, civil society fosters a sense of collective agency, empowering citizens to contribute to the broader vision of a democratic Eritrea.

Women's Empowerment Initiatives:

Recognizing the pivotal role of women in societal transformation, civil society places a strong emphasis on women's empowerment initiatives. Organizations work towards gender equality, advocate for women's rights, and create spaces for women to actively participate in decision-making processes. The inclusion of women becomes integral to the vision of a truly representative and inclusive democracy.

Networking and Collaboration:

Civil society organizations understand the strength in unity and actively engage in networking and collaboration. Partnerships between organizations, both within Eritrea and on the international stage, amplify their collective impact. Collaborative efforts ensure a coordinated approach, maximizing resources, and enhancing the effectiveness of advocacy campaigns for democratic reforms.

Defiance in the Face of Repression:

Civil society faces various forms of repression in the pursuit of democratic values. Despite challenges, these organizations demonstrate remarkable resilience and defiance. Their commitment to the principles of democracy and human rights remains unwavering, even in the face of government intimidation, censorship, and attempts to stifle their advocacy.

Diaspora Connections:

The Eritrean diaspora becomes an integral part of civil society efforts, leveraging its global reach to amplify the call for democratic reforms. Diaspora-based organizations collaborate with those within the country, creating transnational networks that bridge experiences, resources, and strategies for advocacy. The diaspora's role underscores the interconnectedness of Eritrean communities worldwide in the pursuit of democratic ideals.

This chapter explores the indispensable role of civil society in Eritrea's journey towards democratic reforms, shedding light on the multifaceted contributions, challenges faced, and the resilience demonstrated by organizations committed to shaping a more just and democratic future.

8.3 International Solidarity

Diplomatic Support for Democratic Transition:

The call for democratic reforms in Eritrea finds resonance on the international stage as governments, and diplomatic entities express solidarity with the aspirations of the Eritrean people. Diplomatic support becomes a crucial pillar, with nations recognizing the importance of a peaceful and democratic transition for the stability and prosperity of the Horn of Africa region.

Human Rights Advocacy:

International human rights organizations and advocates join forces with their Eritrean counterparts, amplifying the call for democratic reforms. Through reports, advocacy campaigns, and engagement with international bodies, these entities shine a spotlight on human rights abuses, contributing to global awareness and mobilizing support for the protection of fundamental freedoms.

Diplomatic Pressure for Reform:

Governments and international organizations exert diplomatic pressure on the Eritrean government to initiate democratic reforms. This pressure manifests through statements, resolutions, and diplomatic channels that emphasize the international community's expectation for a transition towards democratic governance, respect for human rights, and adherence to the rule of law.

Sanctions and Incentives:

The international community utilizes targeted sanctions and incentives to encourage positive changes within Eritrea. Sanctions may be employed as a tool to address human rights violations and undemocratic practices, while incentives, such as development aid and trade partnerships, are leveraged to encourage the government's commitment to democratic reforms and the improvement of human rights conditions.

Mediation and Conflict Resolution:

International organizations and diplomatic entities actively engage in mediation and conflict resolution efforts to address internal tensions and conflicts within Eritrea. Facilitating dialogue between the government and various stakeholders, these mediation initiatives aim to create a conducive environment for democratic reforms and the resolution of longstanding issues.

Support for Civil Society:

International solidarity extends to support for Eritrean civil society organizations actively advocating for democratic reforms. Funding, training, and collaboration with international counterparts strengthen the capacity of these organizations, enabling them to play a more robust role in promoting democratic values, human rights, and transparent governance.

Diplomatic Recognition of Opposition:

Governments and international bodies consider diplomatic recognition of opposition movements or alternative governance structures that align with democratic principles. This recognition serves as a diplomatic signal of support for democratic aspirations and a commitment to engaging with entities that represent the will of the Eritrean people.

Regional Collaboration:

International solidarity extends to regional collaboration, with neighboring countries and regional organizations actively engaging in efforts to support democratic transitions in Eritrea. Regional stability is recognized as interconnected with Eritrea's political landscape, prompting collaborative initiatives that promote democratic governance, conflict resolution, and economic development.

Peacekeeping and Security Assistance:

International organizations provide peacekeeping and security assistance to ensure a stable environment conducive to democratic reforms. Support in the form of peacekeeping missions, security sector reform, and capacity-building initiatives aims to address security challenges, creating the conditions necessary for a peaceful transition and the establishment of democratic institutions.

Election Monitoring and Observers:

International organizations and entities specializing in election monitoring and observation actively participate in the democratic transition process. Their presence contributes to the transparency of electoral processes, assuring the international community and Eritreans that elections are conducted in a fair and democratic manner, free from manipulation or coercion.

This chapter explores the role of international solidarity in supporting Eritrea's journey toward democratic reforms. From diplomatic engagement to advocacy and practical assistance, the global community's solidarity reflects a shared commitment to democratic values and the collective aspirations of the Eritrean people.

8.4 Rebuilding Democratic Institutions

Transparent Electoral Processes:

A cornerstone of rebuilding democratic institutions in Eritrea is the establishment of transparent electoral processes. Independent electoral commissions, free from political interference, are instituted to oversee fair and inclusive elections. Measures such as voter education, equal access to media, and international election monitoring ensure the credibility of the electoral system.

Separation of Powers:

The rebuilding process prioritizes the separation of powers to prevent the concentration of authority. Constitutional reforms define clear roles for the executive, legislative, and judicial branches, fostering a system of checks and balances. Independent judiciary bodies are established to uphold the rule of law and protect citizens' rights.

Constitutional Reforms:

Eritrea embarks on a comprehensive process of constitutional reforms, engaging citizens in discussions to shape the guiding principles of the nation. The new constitution enshrines democratic values, human rights, and the aspirations of a diverse society. It becomes a living document that reflects the evolving needs and expectations of the Eritrean people.

Independent Media and Freedom of Expression:

The rebuilding of democratic institutions includes a vibrant and independent media landscape. Legal frameworks are established to safeguard freedom of expression, and media organizations operate without fear of censorship. A diverse range of voices, representing various perspectives, contributes to a well-informed public discourse that is essential for a thriving democracy.

Civil Service Reform:

To ensure the professionalism and non-partisanship of government institutions, civil service reform becomes a priority. Merit-based recruitment, transparent promotion processes, and ongoing training programs contribute to the development of a capable and accountable civil service. Public servants become dedicated to serving the interests of the people rather than a political agenda.

Local Governance and Decentralization:

Rebuilding democratic institutions involves empowering local communities through decentralized governance structures. Local government bodies are strengthened, allowing for greater citizen participation in decision-making processes. Decentralization fosters a sense of ownership and accountability at the community level, addressing the diverse needs of Eritrean society.

Anti-Corruption Measures:

A robust anti-corruption framework is implemented to safeguard the integrity of democratic institutions. Independent anti-corruption bodies investigate allegations of corruption, and measures are put in place to promote transparency in public administration. By addressing corruption, Eritrea creates an environment conducive to trust in governmental institutions.

Inclusive Policies for Minorities:

Recognizing the diversity within the nation, inclusive policies are adopted to address the rights and representation of minority groups. Affirmative action programs and policies that promote cultural diversity contribute to a more inclusive and representative democracy, ensuring that the interests of all citizens are considered in the decision-making process.

Truth and Reconciliation Commission:

As part of rebuilding democratic institutions, a Truth and Reconciliation Commission is established. The commission provides a platform for acknowledging historical injustices, documenting human rights violations, and fostering reconciliation among communities. By addressing the wounds of the past, Eritrea paves the way for a united and resilient nation.

International Collaboration in Institution Building:

Eritrea actively collaborates with the international community in the process of rebuilding democratic institutions. Partnerships with international organizations, governments, and experts contribute to capacity-building, knowledge exchange, and the implementation of best practices. This collaborative approach ensures that Eritrea benefits from global experiences in institution building.

As Eritrea undergoes the profound task of rebuilding democratic institutions, this chapter explores the key components of the transformation process, examining the principles, reforms, and collaborative efforts that shape a democratic and resilient future for the nation.

8.5 Empowering Communities

Community-Led Development Initiatives:

Empowering communities in Eritrea involves fostering community-led development initiatives. Local residents actively participate in identifying priorities, designing projects, and implementing solutions that address their unique needs. This approach ensures that development is tailored to the specific circumstances and aspirations of each community.

Capacity-Building Programs:

Empowerment is facilitated through capacity-building programs that provide community members with the skills and knowledge needed to actively engage in the development process. Workshops, training sessions, and educational programs focus on areas such as leadership, project management, and sustainable practices, enhancing the capacity of individuals to contribute meaningfully to their communities.

Inclusive Decision-Making Processes:

Empowering communities entails establishing inclusive decision-making processes. Local governance structures are designed to facilitate the active participation of community members, including marginalized groups and women, in decision-making. Participatory forums, town hall meetings, and community assemblies become spaces where diverse voices are heard and where consensus is built on matters affecting the community.

Access to Information and Resources:

Ensuring access to information and resources is fundamental to community empowerment. Transparent communication channels are established, providing communities with timely and relevant information about development projects, government initiatives, and available resources. Access to resources, including education, healthcare, and economic opportunities, is democratized to promote inclusivity.

Strengthening Social Cohesion:

Community empowerment involves fostering social cohesion and a sense of shared identity. Initiatives that celebrate cultural diversity, traditions, and local heritage contribute to a strong social fabric. By building connections and understanding among community members, social cohesion becomes a resilient foundation for collective action and mutual support.

Women’s and Youth Empowerment:

Special attention is given to the empowerment of women and youth, recognizing their unique roles in community development. Programs aimed at women's economic empowerment, education, and leadership opportunities create pathways for increased participation. Youth empowerment initiatives focus on education, skill development, and mentorship, nurturing the next generation of community leaders.

Sustainable Agriculture and Livelihoods:

Empowering communities includes supporting sustainable agriculture and livelihoods. Agricultural practices that prioritize environmental conservation, water efficiency, and biodiversity contribute to long-term food security. Economic opportunities in sectors such as eco-tourism, handicrafts, and small-scale enterprises provide diverse avenues for community members to improve their livelihoods.

Healthcare and Education Accessibility:

Community empowerment addresses barriers to healthcare and education by improving accessibility. Health clinics, schools, and educational resources are strategically placed to ensure that all community members, including those in remote areas, have access to essential services. Health and education campaigns promote awareness and preventive measures, empowering individuals to take charge of their well-being.

Disaster Preparedness and Resilience:

Building community resilience involves implementing disaster preparedness programs. Communities are equipped with the knowledge and resources to respond effectively to natural disasters and emergencies. Early warning systems, community drills, and collaborative efforts with local authorities enhance the resilience of communities in the face of environmental challenges.

Microfinance and Economic Cooperatives:

Empowering communities economically involves the establishment of microfinance initiatives and economic cooperatives. These entities provide financial support, training, and resources to local entrepreneurs, enabling the development of small businesses and cooperative ventures. Economic empowerment at the community level contributes to poverty reduction and sustainable development.

This chapter explores the diverse strategies and initiatives employed to empower communities in Eritrea, emphasizing the importance of community-led development, inclusive decision-making, and sustainable practices as foundational elements for a resilient and vibrant nation.

8.6 Truth and Reconciliation

Acknowledging Historical Injustices:

The Truth and Reconciliation process in Eritrea begins with a courageous acknowledgment of historical injustices. Individuals and communities come forward to share their experiences, ensuring that the full scope of past wrongs is brought to light. This acknowledgment becomes a collective act of courage and a crucial step toward healing.

Documentation of Human Rights Violations:

A central aspect of Truth and Reconciliation is the documentation of human rights violations. Independent commissions work meticulously to compile a comprehensive record of past abuses, including cases of torture, disappearances, and repression. The documentation process serves as a testament to the suffering endured by individuals and communities, validating their experiences.

Victim-Centered Approach:

The Truth and Reconciliation Commission adopts a victim-centered approach, prioritizing the voices and experiences of those who have suffered. Victims are provided with a platform to share their stories, ensuring that their narratives are heard and respected. Support services, including counseling and legal assistance, are offered to address the emotional and practical needs of survivors.

Perpetrator Accountability:

While fostering a culture of reconciliation, the Truth and Reconciliation process also addresses accountability for perpetrators of human rights abuses. Mechanisms are put in place to ensure that those responsible for grave violations are held accountable. This may involve legal proceedings, truth-telling, and acknowledgment of responsibility as part of the broader reconciliation efforts.

Community Healing Initiatives:

Beyond individual healing, Truth and Reconciliation extends to healing at the community level. Community-based initiatives, facilitated by the Commission, bring together individuals from diverse backgrounds to engage in dialogue, share perspectives, and build bridges of understanding. These initiatives aim to repair social fabric and foster a sense of unity among different communities.

Apology and Reparations:

As a gesture of acknowledgment and accountability, the government issues public apologies for historical injustices. Reparation programs are established to address the material and symbolic needs of victims. These may include compensation, access to education and healthcare, and initiatives to restore dignity and support the rebuilding of affected communities.

National Memorialization:

The Truth and Reconciliation process culminates in national memorialization efforts. Memorials and commemorative events are established to honor the memory of those who suffered, ensuring that the nation collectively remembers its painful past. These memorials become spaces for reflection, remembrance, and a commitment to a shared future free from the traumas of the past.

Educational Curriculum Reform:

To foster a culture of understanding and reconciliation, educational curricula undergo reform. The history taught in schools reflects a more comprehensive and accurate narrative, encompassing the diverse experiences of Eritrean communities. Educational programs emphasize tolerance, respect for diversity, and the importance of human rights.

Diaspora Engagement in Reconciliation:

The Eritrean diaspora actively engages in Truth and Reconciliation efforts. Diaspora communities participate in initiatives that promote dialogue, memorialization, and acknowledgment of historical injustices. Transnational collaboration becomes a powerful force in fostering reconciliation, connecting the experiences of those within Eritrea and those abroad.

Future-Oriented Reconciliation:

Truth and Reconciliation in Eritrea is forward-looking, emphasizing the importance of learning from the past to shape a positive future. The process instills a commitment to democratic values, human rights, and the prevention of future abuses. Reconciliation becomes a dynamic and ongoing journey toward a just and inclusive society.

In exploring Truth and Reconciliation in Eritrea, this chapter delves into the profound process of acknowledging historical injustices, fostering healing at individual and community levels, and building a foundation for a shared future grounded in truth, justice, and reconciliation.

8.7 Economic Development and Social Justice

Inclusive Economic Policies:

Eritrea's pursuit of economic development is guided by inclusive policies that prioritize social justice. The government implements measures to address economic disparities, ensuring that the benefits of development reach all segments of society. Inclusive economic policies focus on poverty reduction, job creation, and equitable distribution of resources.

Job Creation and Skill Development:

A key component of economic development is the creation of employment opportunities and skill development programs. The government invests in sectors that have the potential to generate jobs, such as infrastructure, agriculture, and technology. Skill development initiatives equip the workforce with the necessary competencies to participate meaningfully in the evolving economy.

Social Safety Nets:

To protect vulnerable populations, social safety nets are established. Welfare programs, healthcare coverage, and education subsidies contribute to social justice by providing a safety net for those facing economic challenges. These safety nets aim to prevent the perpetuation of poverty and ensure that all citizens have access to essential services.

Sustainable Development Initiatives:

Economic development is approached with a commitment to sustainability. Initiatives focus on environmentally conscious practices, renewable energy, and conservation efforts. Sustainable development ensures that economic growth does not compromise the well-being of future generations and reflects a commitment to responsible stewardship of natural resources.

Access to Financial Services:

Social justice is promoted through initiatives that enhance access to financial services, particularly for marginalized communities. Microfinance programs, community banking, and financial literacy initiatives empower individuals to start businesses, invest in education, and improve their economic circumstances. Financial inclusion becomes a cornerstone of social and economic justice.

Gender Equality in the Economy:

Eritrea actively promotes gender equality in the economic sphere. Policies are implemented to address gender-based discrimination, ensure equal pay for equal work, and create an environment where women can thrive in the workforce. Economic empowerment programs for women contribute to breaking down barriers and fostering a more inclusive economy.

Affordable Housing:

Social justice is advanced through the provision of affordable housing solutions. Government initiatives aim to address housing challenges, particularly for low-income families. Affordable housing programs contribute to creating stable communities and improving living standards for all citizens.

Education for All:

Access to quality education is central to Eritrea's commitment to social justice. The government invests in education infrastructure, teacher training, and curriculum development to ensure that all citizens, regardless of socio-economic background, have access to a quality education. Education becomes a tool for empowerment and social mobility.

Universal Healthcare:

Eritrea endeavors to achieve universal healthcare, ensuring that every citizen has access to essential medical services. Healthcare reforms focus on preventive care, infrastructure development, and the training of healthcare professionals. The goal is to create a healthcare system that prioritizes the well-being of all citizens and promotes social justice.

Community-Based Development:

Social justice is woven into the fabric of community-based development initiatives. Local communities actively participate in the planning and implementation of development projects, ensuring that the unique needs of each community are addressed. Community-based development becomes a model for participatory governance and equitable resource distribution.

Corporate Social Responsibility:

Businesses operating in Eritrea are encouraged to embrace corporate social responsibility

(CSR). Companies contribute to social justice by investing in local communities, supporting education and healthcare initiatives, and minimizing their environmental impact. CSR becomes a collaborative effort between the public and private sectors to create a socially responsible and sustainable economy.

This chapter explores how Eritrea's approach to economic development is intertwined with principles of social justice. By prioritizing inclusivity, sustainability, and the well-being of all citizens, the nation seeks to build an economy that serves as a foundation for a just and equitable society.

8.8 Diaspora Engagement and Return

Transnational Collaboration:

Eritrea actively engages its diaspora as a valuable resource for national development. Transnational collaboration involves leveraging the skills, expertise, and resources of Eritreans living abroad to contribute to the country's growth. Collaborative initiatives encompass economic development, education, healthcare, and various sectors critical to the nation's well-being.

Investment and Entrepreneurship:

The Eritrean diaspora plays a pivotal role in economic development through investments and entrepreneurship. Diaspora members invest in businesses, startups, and development projects that contribute to job creation and economic growth. Entrepreneurial ventures initiated by the diaspora become catalysts for innovation and diversification of the national economy.

Knowledge Transfer and Capacity Building:

Diaspora engagement focuses on knowledge transfer and capacity building. Programs are established to facilitate the transfer of skills, expertise, and technological know-how from the diaspora to local communities. Workshops, mentorship programs, and collaborative projects ensure that the wealth of knowledge within the diaspora is harnessed for the benefit of Eritrea.

Education and Research Collaborations:

The diaspora contributes to educational advancements and research collaborations.

Partnerships between diaspora academics, researchers, and local institutions foster innovation and academic excellence. Exchange programs, joint research projects, and scholarship initiatives strengthen Eritrea's educational landscape and position the country within the global knowledge community.

Healthcare Initiatives:

Diaspora engagement extends to healthcare initiatives, with healthcare professionals in the diaspora collaborating with local counterparts. Medical missions, training programs, and the sharing of medical expertise contribute to improving healthcare infrastructure and addressing public health challenges. The diaspora becomes a valuable asset in building a robust and responsive healthcare system.

Cultural and Artistic Contributions:

Cultural and artistic contributions from the diaspora enrich Eritrea's cultural landscape. Diaspora artists, musicians, writers, and cultural practitioners collaborate with local counterparts to showcase the richness of Eritrean heritage. Cultural exchange programs and artistic initiatives become bridges that connect diverse Eritrean communities worldwide.

Advocacy for Democratic Reforms:

The diaspora remains actively involved in advocating for democratic reforms in Eritrea. Diaspora communities organize awareness campaigns, engage in lobbying efforts, and collaborate with international organizations to amplify the voices of those seeking political change. The diaspora's role in advocating for human rights and democratic values contributes to a global movement for positive change.

Return and Reintegration Programs:

Eritrea implements return and reintegration programs to facilitate the voluntary return of diaspora members who wish to contribute directly to the country's development. These programs provide support in areas such as housing, employment, and cultural adaptation, easing the process of reintegration for returnees who bring with them valuable skills and experiences.

Diaspora Philanthropy and Social Initiatives:

Diaspora philanthropy becomes a driving force behind social initiatives in Eritrea. Charitable organizations and community-based projects supported by the diaspora address social challenges, including poverty alleviation, education, and healthcare. The diaspora's commitment to social initiatives reflects a shared responsibility for the well-being of Eritrean communities.

Strengthening National Identity:

Diaspora engagement contributes to the strengthening of national identity. Cultural exchanges, language programs, and collaborative projects foster a sense of unity and shared identity among Eritreans across the globe. The diaspora becomes an integral part of shaping and preserving the cultural fabric that defines Eritrea.

This chapter explores the dynamic relationship between Eritrea and its diaspora, highlighting the collaborative efforts that contribute to economic development, cultural enrichment, and the pursuit of democratic values. The engagement of the diaspora emerges as a powerful force for positive change and national development.

8.9 Cultural Renaissance and Intellectual Freedom

Revitalizing Cultural Heritage:

Eritrea embarks on a cultural renaissance, celebrating and revitalizing its rich cultural heritage. Cultural institutions, festivals, and programs are established to preserve and promote traditional arts, music, dance, and literature. Initiatives that showcase the diversity of Eritrean cultures contribute to a sense of pride and identity among the population.

Language and Literature Promotion:

The promotion of Eritrean languages and literature became a cornerstone of the cultural renaissance. Initiatives are launched to support the development and publication of literature in local languages, ensuring that diverse voices and stories are shared. Literary festivals, poetry readings, and writing workshops create spaces for intellectual expression and creativity.

Freedom of Expression and Media Pluralism:

Eritrea embraces a commitment to intellectual freedom by promoting freedom of expression and media pluralism. Reforms in media laws facilitate the establishment of independent media outlets, creating a diverse and vibrant media landscape. Journalists and writers have the freedom to explore diverse perspectives and contribute to informed public discourse.

Academic Freedom and Research:

Academic freedom is championed, allowing scholars and researchers to explore a wide range of topics without fear of censorship. Research institutions and universities become hubs of intellectual inquiry, fostering an environment where critical thinking and open dialogue are encouraged. Collaboration with international academic institutions enhances the global exchange of knowledge.

Cultural Exchanges and Collaboration:

Eritrea actively engages in cultural exchanges and collaborations with international partners. Artist residencies, exchange programs, and collaborative projects bring together Eritrean and international artists, writers, and intellectuals. These initiatives contribute to a cross-cultural dialogue that enriches the intellectual landscape and fosters a global appreciation for Eritrean creativity.

Public Lectures and Intellectual Forums:

Public lectures, intellectual forums, and panel discussions become regular features of the cultural and intellectual scene in Eritrea. Renowned thinkers, academics, and artists are invited to share their insights and engage with the public on a variety of topics. These forums create spaces for intellectual exchange and the exploration of new ideas.

Museums and Cultural Institutions:

Museums and cultural institutions are established or revitalized to showcase Eritrea's history, art, and cultural achievements. These spaces become hubs for education and reflection, inviting the public to connect with their heritage and fostering a sense of pride in the nation's cultural accomplishments.

Support for Artists and Creatives:

Eritrea invests in supporting artists and creatives through grants, residencies, and cultural programs. Recognizing the role of the arts in expressing diverse perspectives, capturing historical narratives, and fostering creativity, the government actively supports the work of artists and ensures their contribution to the cultural renaissance.

Intellectual Property Protection:

The protection of intellectual property becomes a priority, ensuring that artists, writers, and creators are acknowledged and rewarded for their contributions. Intellectual property laws are strengthened to safeguard the rights of individuals and encourage a flourishing creative industry.

Open Dialogues on Controversial Issues:

Eritrea promotes open dialogues on controversial issues, encouraging discussions on topics that were previously considered sensitive. Public debates and conversations on political, social, and cultural matters contribute to a climate of intellectual freedom, where diverse viewpoints are respected and considered.

International Collaboration in Arts and Culture:

Eritrea actively collaborates with international partners in the arts and culture sector. Exchange programs, joint exhibitions, and collaborative projects with artists and institutions from around the world foster a global perspective and position Eritrea within the broader context of the international cultural community.

This chapter explores Eritrea's commitment to a cultural renaissance and intellectual freedom, emphasizing the importance of preserving heritage, promoting diverse expressions, and creating an environment where intellectual inquiry and artistic creativity thrive.

8.10 International Collaboration for Sustainable Development

Sustainable Development Goals (SDGs) Alignment:

Eritrea actively aligns its national development agenda with the United Nations Sustainable Development Goals (SDGs). The government commits to achieving specific targets related to poverty reduction, education, healthcare, gender equality, and environmental sustainability. This alignment facilitates international collaboration and positions Eritrea as a global partner in sustainable development.

Multilateral Partnerships:

Eritrea engages in multilateral partnerships with international organizations such as the United Nations, World Bank, and regional development banks. These partnerships provide financial support, technical expertise, and capacity-building initiatives that contribute to the implementation of sustainable development projects. Collaborative efforts focus on areas such as infrastructure development, healthcare, and education.

Bilateral Cooperation:

Bilateral cooperation agreements are established with partner countries that share common goals in sustainable development. These agreements encompass economic cooperation, trade partnerships, and joint initiatives in areas such as agriculture, technology transfer, and renewable energy. Bilateral collaboration enhances Eritrea's capacity to address complex challenges and leverage international expertise.

Foreign Aid and Development Assistance:

Eritrea receives foreign aid and development assistance from donor countries committed to supporting sustainable development. These funds are directed towards projects that address poverty, improve healthcare and education, promote gender equality, and enhance environmental sustainability. Development assistance plays a crucial role in accelerating progress towards national development goals.

Technology Transfer and Innovation:

International collaboration facilitates the transfer of technology and innovative solutions to address developmental challenges. Partnerships with technologically advanced countries and institutions support Eritrea in adopting sustainable practices, improving agricultural techniques, and embracing advancements in healthcare and education. Technology transfer becomes a catalyst for accelerated development.

Climate Change Mitigation and Adaptation:

Eritrea collaborates with international partners on climate change mitigation and adaptation initiatives. Projects focus on sustainable land management, renewable energy, and resilience-building measures to address the impacts of climate change. International collaboration strengthens Eritrea's capacity to navigate environmental challenges and promotes sustainable practices.

Cross-Border Initiatives:

Eritrea actively engages in cross-border initiatives with neighboring countries to address shared challenges and promote regional stability. Collaborative efforts may include joint infrastructure projects, coordinated responses to health emergencies, and initiatives that foster economic integration. Cross-border collaboration contributes to a more interconnected and sustainable regional landscape.

Cultural and Educational Exchanges:

International collaboration extends to cultural and educational exchanges, promoting a global perspective and cross-cultural understanding.

Eritrean students and professionals participate in exchange programs, while international scholars and artists contribute to the nation's cultural and intellectual landscape. These exchanges foster a rich tapestry of ideas and experiences.

Disaster Preparedness and Humanitarian Assistance:

Eritrea collaborates with international organizations and donor countries to enhance disaster preparedness and provide humanitarian assistance in times of crisis. Partnerships focus on building resilience, improving early warning systems, and ensuring swift and effective responses to natural disasters and emergencies.

Monitoring and Evaluation Framework:

A robust monitoring and evaluation framework is established to assess the impact of international collaboration on sustainable development. Regular assessments and feedback mechanisms ensure that collaborative efforts align with national priorities, are effective in achieving desired outcomes, and contribute to the overall well-being of Eritrean communities.

This chapter explores Eritrea's commitment to international collaboration for sustainable development, emphasizing partnerships with global entities, donor countries, and regional neighbors. The collaborative efforts outlined contribute to the nation's progress in achieving sustainable development goals and fostering a resilient and prosperous future.

Endnotes:

As we draw the curtains on this narrative of resilience and change, it is imperative to reflect on the profound stories shared within these pages. The journey chronicled here is not just a collection of events but a testament to the unwavering spirit and determination of the Eritrean people.

Throughout this exploration of Eritrea's enduring struggle for change, we've encountered tales of courage, sacrifice, and unwavering hope. Behind each account lies the heartbeat of a nation, pulsating with a fervent desire for progress and transformation.

The stories recounted within this book are mere glimpses into a larger narrative—a narrative shaped by countless individuals, communities, and generations who have contributed their unwavering efforts toward a shared vision of a better tomorrow.

In closing, we extend our deepest gratitude to all those who generously shared their experiences, insights, and perspectives. Their willingness to open their hearts and recount their journeys has enriched this narrative immeasurably.

We also express heartfelt appreciation to the researchers, historians, and individuals whose dedication to preserving the history and culture of Eritrea has been invaluable in shaping this work.

Lastly, to you, the reader, we extend our thanks for embarking on this journey with us. May the spirit of endurance, resilience, and hope portrayed in these pages resonate within you, reminding us all of the profound strength found within the human spirit.

With deep respect and gratitude,

This endnote serves as a final reflection, expressing gratitude to contributors, acknowledging the significance of the journey portrayed in the book, and encouraging readers to carry forward the spirit of resilience and hope embodied in the narrative.

Printed in Great Britain
by Amazon